# It's About Time

Leading School Reform in
an Era of Time Scarcity

## James E. Bruno

CORWIN PRESS, INC.
A Sage Publications Company
Thousand Oaks, California

Copyright © 1997 by Corwin Press, Inc.

*For information:*

Corwin Press, Inc.
A Sage Publications Company
2455 Teller Road
Thousand Oaks, California 91320
E-mail: order@corwin.sagepub.com

SAGE Publications Ltd.
6 Bonhill Street
London EC2A 4PU
United Kingdom

SAGE Publications India Pvt. Ltd.
M-32 Market
Greater Kailash I
New Delhi 110 048 India

Printed in the United States of America

**Library of Congress Cataloging-in-Publication Data**

Bruno, James E.
    It's about time : leading school reform in an era of time scarcity / James E.
Bruno.
        p.  cm.
    Includes bibliographical references and index.
    ISBN 0-8039-6504-4 (cloth : acid-free paper). — ISBN 0-8039-6505-2 (pbk. :
acid-free paper)
    1. Teacher participation in administration—United States. 2. Teachers—Time
management—United States. 3. Educational change—United States.  I. Title.
LB2806.45.B78  1997
    371.2—dc21                                                                   97-21136

This book is printed on acid-free paper.

97  98  99  00  01  02  03  10  9  8  7  6  5  4  3  2  1

Corwin Press Production Editor: S. Marlene Head
Editorial Assistant: Kristen L. Gibson
Typesetters: Laura A. and William C. E. Lawrie
Cover Designer: Marcia M. Rosenburg
Indexer: Mary Kidd

# Contents

# Preface

*In theory one is aware that the earth revolves, but in practice one does not perceive it. So it is with Time in one's life.*

MARCEL PROUST (1913-1927)

As we approach the new millennium, a once-in-a-thousand-years event that will be experienced by most individuals reading this book, the concept of time in a lifetime will take on profound psychological as well as physical significance. This book attempts to examine the former in the context of the latter with specific focus on classroom teachers engaged in the time-consuming efforts of the school reform movement. Although land, labor, and capital dominated thinking with regard to economic growth in the 20th century, land, labor, capital, and time will dominate thinking in the 21st century. In most of the industrialized countries of the world, the words *time* and *money* are often used interchangeably, that is, to save money, to save time, to waste time, to waste money. But as the popular song says, "Money can't buy you love," or as the expression states, "Money isn't everything." After completing extensive research on classroom teachers that resulted in the writing of this book, I have concluded that for many, time usually is or can become far more important than money. But this book isn't about the subject of chronological time itself, or the history of clock time, or even time management. Instead, this book is about the more important leadership perspective of lifetime management with specific reference to the psychosocial construct of time and how it affects the behaviors of classroom teachers in school organizations. Time investment and time perception of classroom teachers in school organizations provide school leaders with an important perspective for the behavior of teachers toward the school reform movement. Teacher participation rates in school reform efforts by a school organization and the attitudes of teachers toward the school change and reform process are extraordinarily time dependent. In addition, classroom teacher behaviors in the school organization such as dropout, burnout, commitment, and pushout are particularly time sensitive. It's *time*, therefore, and not money that seems to be the major impediment for classroom teachers to participate in school reform activities. *Because nearly every report, research article, and book written about the American experience with school reform has underscored the problem of time as being the major obstacle to the change process, the concept of time takes on immense applied as well as theoretical significance for school leaders and educational researchers.* It's About Time attempts to explore the following issues from the perspective of both the classroom teacher and school organization:

1. Why time and time sensitivity are so important to the management of the change and reform process in the school organization
2. How time is associated with behavior and participation by classroom teachers in the change and reform activities in the school organization
3. What time-selective effective leadership and incentive strategies are needed to enhance classroom teacher participation in school reform and change activities

As previously noted, this book is not about time management or the various methods that school organizations can use to structure and manage the time of its classroom teachers more efficiently. Instead, this book presents a psychosocial perspective of time and the problems it presents both for teachers in terms of their personal quest for attaining lifetime goals (i.e., lifetime management) and for educational leaders in terms of their management of the change and reform process in the school organization (i.e., leadership in an era of time scarcity). *It's About Time,* therefore, is primarily directed at educational leaders, especially school principals and their assistants, school supervisors, subject matter specialists, and central office administrators. Preservice and inservice classroom teachers, however, should also find this book extremely useful because it articulates and presents insights regarding the important role that time plays in the lifetimes and careers of teachers. To a lesser extent, this book can also be extremely useful for school board members who have to understand the concept of time as a currency of exchange between the classroom teacher and the school organization. With these overall objectives in mind, this book limits the scope of its analysis to examining only those specific time-related concepts that are directly associated with classroom teachers and the change and reform process in school organizations. Special attention is given to the school change and reform process as practiced in K-12 public school organizations. What makes the subject of time and teacher participation in school reform efforts so difficult, but interesting, to examine is that the perception and value of time is not the same for all teachers. The largest difference in participation by classroom teachers is associated with age. This book attempts to explain why, using the psychosocial perspective of time.

---

Time perception affects much of our professional and personal decision making in life, which, in turn, affects our observed behaviors in social organizations.

---

As an educational researcher, I have always felt that there was an important need to examine core human values of teachers that underlie their behavior in the classroom. There are many professional, personal, demographic, and cultural variables that affect classroom teacher behavior in the school organization, but a teacher's orientation to time is perhaps the most important. Time perception affects much of our professional and personal decision making in life, which, in turn, affects our observed behaviors in social organizations. Because understanding the important time linkages between teachers and school organizations in the context of school reform is so significant to educational management, this book might also be considered a first step in understanding time and the management of the change process in school organizations. Change is probably one of the most difficult tasks for any individual to accomplish. Change threatens most individuals because it forces one to behave in an unfamiliar way. Change, by definition, requires behavioral changes in classroom teacher practices and additional time investment not only to learn about the change but to actually deliver the change to the classroom.

---

School organizational leadership in an era of time scarcity, therefore, becomes a serious test of management and skill because it affects a core human value of classroom teachers, namely, the use of time and the control over time.

---

The central issue, from a teacher perspective, is that school change and reform implies significant amounts of "extra" after-school time, not extra student contact time commitment. Unless time is taken from students, this extra time can only come from the finite amount of time that is available in a teacher's lifetime. The multitude of other, outside-of-school, time-consuming activities that are present in a teacher's life places school reform time in direct competition with lifestyle satisfaction time. Because of the unique perspective and point of view taken in this book with regard to teacher time, both strong disagreement and agreement among classroom teachers and school administrative personnel will be generated. Who actually controls the time of a classroom teacher is extremely controversial. Providing opportunities for discussion, eliciting differing points of view, encouraging spirited debate, and having disagreements, therefore, are essential for meeting some of the objectives of this book—namely, to inform, engineer, enlighten, and suggest, regarding the psychosocial construct of time. To help attain these goals, the end of each chapter includes discussion and point-of-view questions. This feature of the book permits school leaders to elicit from their classroom teachers their own personal values, insights, and feelings about how some of these time constructs affect their own particular life. In essence, the discussion of ideas presented in this book is meant to increase the time sensitivity of school leaders and teachers concerning what is quickly becoming recognized as a fundamental resource and currency of exchange in both the life processes of the classroom teacher and evolutionary processes of the school organization. The following five major time concepts and temporal orientations are explored in various chapters:

1. *Time investment portfolios,* or the way hours in a lifetime are invested by classroom teachers to attain their personal goals in life, that is, lifestyle satisfaction, happiness, self-actualization. These time investments define the persona of the classroom teacher and later in life the nature of the "self" with regard to lifestyle satisfaction.

2. *Temporal orientation or temporal dominance,* or the way classroom teachers orient themselves toward the past, present, and future, that is, the role of memory and vision and their impact on present behavior in the classroom and in the school organization.

3. *Sense of time passage,* or the way each hour of time is subjectively weighted over the career of a classroom teacher, that is, the value or the psychological worth of time for a teacher as he or she ages in the school organization. This concept describes the perceived value of time over a career span of a classroom teacher.

4. *Engagement and participation motivation,* or the ratio of benefits or satisfaction derived to time effort expended for a particular time-consuming activity, that is, what motivates teachers to participate and in engage in the multitude of reform and change activities of the school organization. Benefits can be monetary, social, professional, or personal in nature, and time efforts can be related to convenience as well as both the qualitative and quantitative dimensions of time.

5. *Time clock orientation,* or the type of overall time pattern that individual teachers and school organizations use to orient and pace their activities. Stated differently, the conflicts that emerge when the cyclical time clock of the school organization interacts with the linear time clock of the classroom teacher. These different views of time passage generate differing expectations with regard to time investments and typically result in time conflict between classroom teachers and the school organization.

The specific purpose of the book, therefore, is to explore the impact of each of these five time concepts on the lives of classroom teachers and the school organizations they work in. Finally, implications for classroom teachers regarding their time sensitivity, time investment, and time perceptions are developed, and strategies for educational leaders of school reform efforts in an era of time scarcity are then presented. To attain these intended objectives, the following organization is used in this book. Chapter 1 examines how teachers' participation in the school reform movement can be viewed from the perspective of time. Special emphasis in this chapter is given to the role that time, energy, and purpose play in the school change and reform process. Insights are then provided concerning the question of why teachers seem to stampede toward change in the abstract, but then stroll toward action in the context of their own classroom. Chapter 2 examines the various psychosocial components or constructs of time and explores their impact on classroom teacher behaviors. This chapter introduces the reader to important time constructs such as temporal orientation, time investment, and the sense or feel of time passage. These time orientation constructs are then described in terms of their association with the change and reform process in school organizations. Chapter 3 focuses complete attention on the role of time in the lifetimes of classroom teachers or, stated differently, the lifetime management of teachers. This chapter attempts to describe teachers in terms of their time investments and temporal orientation over the course of their career in the classroom. The role that time plays in earning a living and the ways the perception of time changes in teachers at midlife and in late career are also explored. Finally, how teachers make choices about their participation in school reform and change activities is also examined in the context of the time needs for defining the persona of a classroom teacher and the time needs for the development of the self, or lifestyle satisfaction. Chapter 4 is directed at establishing the important relationship between time and teacher productivity from the perspective of the school organization. How school organizations structure the resource of time provided by classroom teachers from minutes in the classroom to decades over a teaching career is given particular attention. Chapter 5 examines the linkage or the currency of exchange between teacher time and school organization time. This chapter examines conflict and congruence between teacher and organizational time, and then explores resulting classroom teacher behaviors such as commitment, burnout, pushout, and dropout. Leadership suggestions for getting teachers to pull together, in time and in the school organization, are also provided. Chapter 6 provides recommendations for school leaders with regard to putting their organization in "prime time." Time-sensitive strategies for getting teacher commitment instead of teacher burnout and specific time-sensitive recommendations for the management of the change and reform process are also presented.

> Time quality, or happiness and lifestyle satisfaction, in the lifetime of a teacher probably has much more to do with learning by students than with teacher participation in school reform and change activities.

*It's About Time* is a book that recognizes that leadership in an era of time scarcity has to be extremely sensitive to the time quality of a classroom teacher. Time quality, or happiness and lifestyle satisfaction, in the lifetime of a teacher probably has much more to do with learning by students than with teacher participation in school reform and change activities. In essence, no amount of school reform or change can overcome the dangers posed to students and classroom learning by time-stressed, uncaring, burned-out, insensitive classroom teachers who don't have time for their students or who are unhappy with their lifestyle because of a lack of time control. The concept of time, as explored in this book, therefore, presents the reader with an important interconnecting dynamic of school reform and change efforts in the context of the lifetime of classroom teachers and the evolution of school organizations.

## Acknowledgments

"Live every day as if it were your last—live every day as if you were to live forever" is an important principle for living a full and balanced life. It describes how time is used by individuals in the artistry of living. In the same way artists use color pigments to define artistry on a canvas, the time and time investments of individuals define lifestyle artistry over a lifetime. To professors who teach this important principle to future teachers, to teachers who teach this principle to their students, and to parents who teach this principle to their children, this book is dedicated.

Very few ideas in life are original—we all stand on the shoulders of brilliant men and women who take us to a point in "time" where we can then add our contribution. One such person is Ephraim Ben Baruch from Ben Gurion University in Israel. His brilliant insights, wisdom, and clarity of thinking were a constant source of inspiration to me and a stimulus to my research efforts on time. Ephraim gave me much of his time out of his lifetime. From his gift of time came the idea for this book.

I hope some of the insights presented in this book will transmit the time gift to other individuals so that they might pursue research into this fascinating component of human behavior. This book, therefore, is not only about time but is also dedicated to what time can provide, if invested wisely, to an individual in the course of a lifetime. The wonderful memories of my past with my exceptional mother, Madeline, and my father, John, and to my vision for a future with my wife, Ann, and my wonderful children, Jenny and Julia, were all purchased with the currency of time. Time that was freely given to me by my parents, and time that I presently give to my family, is a currency of life and a nontaxable life resource that yields high dividends toward attaining the goals of lifestyle satisfaction or happiness.

Time and the portfolio of my time investments have formed the fabric of my life and, in a way, have defined both me as a person and my lifetime. As this book suggests, individuals, especially classroom teachers, build and define their lifetimes with their time. Understanding their participation in school reform activities thus becomes a matter of time.

JAMES E. BRUNO

Office: 310-825-8354
E-mail: jbruno@ucla.edu

# About the Author

James E. Bruno teaches and is currently engaged in research at the University of California, Los Angeles, in the areas of educational policy analysis, school administration, school management, and educational planning. The following are his primary research interests.

1. *Quantitative, computer-based decision analysis methods for policy analysis, planning, administration, and management in educational organizations.* Current interests include the use of geographical information (GIS) for evaluating negative and positive effects of geographical space and environments on children and the schooling process.

2. *The development of technology-based formative evaluation and assessment procedures using information-referenced assessment formats with multimedia educational interventions to support instruction.* Current interests include applications of the Information Referenced Testing (IRT) format for supporting and designing individual education plans of action and instructional program support in school and corporate settings.

3. *The study of time, time perceptions, temporal dominance, and time-investment portfolios and their association with student and teacher behaviors in educational organizations.* Current interests include investigating the role that time investment, time perception, and temporal dominance plays in the development of at-risk and resilient behaviors in children.

Bruno has written more than 100 books and articles on various topics dealing with educational policy analysis and planning. In 1992, he was awarded UCLA's EUCLAN prize for educational research having the most impact on urban schools in Los Angeles. Bruno regularly consults to national and international educational agencies, ministries of education, business, and industry in the areas of assessment, decision analysis, geographical mapping, and the linkage between time perceptions and human behavior. He is presently working with the Los Angeles County juvenile court system and the Mathematics in Engineering and Science Achievement (MESA) project of the University of California, office of the president.

# 1

# Stampeding Toward Change, Strolling Toward Action

- Introduction
- Time, Energy, Purpose, and the School Change Process
- Time and Human Behavior With Regard to Change
- Time and the School Reform Movement
- Summary
- Perspectives, Points of View, Discussion

## Introduction

The "currency" that is used to purchase change and reform in school organizations is time.

With the new millennium rapidly approaching, the concept of time and its impact on human behavior will assume added psychological significance. Nowhere will this concept be felt more strongly than among students and their teachers. Not only will students experience this event of a lifetime, but the school organization will have to remind itself about the important linkage between time and change. The last years of the 20th century in U.S. public education have been characterized by immense changes in both the structure and delivery of instruction. The way land, labor, and capital defined economic growth and change in the 20th century, land, labor, capital, and time will define growth and change in the 21st century. The "currency" that is used to purchase change and reform in school organizations is time. It is time derived primarily from the lifetimes of classroom teachers.

From a psychological perspective, change, whether in the workplace or in one's personal life, is probably one of the most difficult tasks for individuals to accomplish. There is always a certain amount of security and time efficiency that is associated with the familiar. To know where everything is, to be familiar with your surroundings, and to do things the same way allows one to develop an important sense of fluency, regularity, and control over time. For leaders of school organizations attempting to motivate professionals such as classroom teachers to change and embrace some of the recommendations of the school reform movement, change in an era of time scarcity becomes a serious test of their leadership skills.

Public organizations, such as schools, have traditionally been difficult to change and reform because there was little economic, legal, and psychological incentive to change. Although most classroom teachers embrace school reform as a concept and as an abstract ideal, many teachers resist it in the specific context of their own classroom. Time scarcity or the unwillingness to provide the resource of time might, therefore, be one of the reasons why teachers stampede toward the school change process as a concept, yet stroll toward change when it specifically affects their classroom. The "why" of this phenomenon seems to be more a psychological reason, associated with teacher perceptions, behavior, and desires in life, than a fiscal one. In fact, comp time or free time is sometimes more valued than extra monetary compensation which may move teachers into a higher income tax level. Because teachers have to change their old, comfortable, convenient, and time-efficient ways of doing things in the classroom, the psychological security and time efficiency associated with familiar ways of doing things are threatened.

---

Educational leaders will have to answer the important question posed by many classroom teachers: "Is the school reform effort worth my added time and effort?"

---

At the core of the psychological resistance to change for classroom teachers is that change implies significant amounts of after-school time or "extra" time will be taken from other time-competing activities in life, such as time for their children, personal health, or older parents. A constant theme throughout this book is that educational leaders will have to effectively answer the most important question posed by many classroom teachers with regard to school reform: "Is the school reform worth my added time and effort?" If the answer to their question is no, or not a strong yes, then the desired school reform and change for that particular teacher will be nearly impossible to attain. The key words are *worth* and *added time*.

Finally, attaining modern change in a school organization is not a one-time event, but an ongoing process. Unlike change and reform in past generations, modern efforts at school change and reform are not "games" devised by school leaders. Once reform is attained, teachers cannot quietly return to their old ways of doing things. The trend for the 21st-century school organization is that all teachers will have to make career-long commitments to the change and reform process. To be effective and long lasting, the agenda for change and reform from the perspective of school leaders will have to be associated with gains or personal worth to the classroom teacher. "Is the reform worth my time?" will have to be placed in the context of a hierarchy of priorities and the various combinations of physical and emotional needs of classroom teachers such as money, power, recognition, professional pride, and personal development. *To base compensation for change and reform solely on a teacher's professional pride or idealism—although admirable and appropriate for some teachers—might exclude reform and change participation by many other teachers in a typical school setting.*

For a substantial number of teachers, time was an important factor in their decision to enter the teaching profession. Classroom teaching is a relatively well-paying, middle-class profession with a 180-day year and a 6- to 7-hour workday schedule at a school site. Suppose school leaders were to impose a school day of 8 a.m. to 5 p.m. with the after-school time period of 3 p.m. to 5 p.m. reserved for planning and staff development to promote change and reform? There would probably be opposition to the plan from all but the most idealistic classroom teachers. Even if teachers were paid for their extra time, there probably would still not be 100% participation.

Many teachers simply want to do something outside of school with what they consider to be *their* time.

This book strongly suggests that school leaders must appreciate and consider the element of time in the lifetimes of teachers as being essential for promoting the school change and reform process. By the word *time*, this book means such psychosocial constructs as time sensitivity, time investment, time orientations, temporal dominance, and time perception. At both the classroom teacher and the school organizational levels, time is the currency of exchange and is, therefore, fundamental to both successful school reform design and its implementation in the classroom. Modern school change is not about teachers simply investing time and doing more of what they presently do, but instead is about teachers investing their time by rethinking basic assumptions about their professional standards of care. For this reason, large time investments by teachers in challenging old assumptions, obtaining new knowledge, and processing this knowledge with action are required. The educational research literature and the research conducted for this book demonstrate that changing behaviors of classroom teachers who have taught for long periods of time under the old system with its antiquated assumptions of student learning is particularly difficult. School change is analogous to losing weight through dieting. The fact that one can be on one diet after another without sustaining the weight loss over time shows that *any change, to be effective, requires an understanding of the relationship between the change process and personal behavior.* Dieting behaviors show the folly of change in weight without taking the time to investigate the basic assumptions that are fundamental to weight loss, namely, changing behavior. Successful weight loss programs aren't attained by diet alone, but are instead a lifelong commitment to a change in individual behavior toward food and exercise. School organizations should follow a similar model for successful reform and change. The fact that many of the needed reforms have not taken hold in schools is nearly fully attributable to teacher behavior not changing because inadequate time was devoted to discussing and thinking about classroom learning. More important, proposed changes are generally not perceived to be worth the added time on the part of the classroom teacher.

There is little doubt that the responsibilities for designing and implementing school reforms and change have primarily fallen on school principals and their support staff of assistants, supervisors, and specialists at the school site. Unfortunately, the "market" incentives available to school leaders to promote change and reform efforts in an era of time scarcity are quite limited. To motivate large groups of professional educators (most with job security) to pull together in time with regard to the change and reform process makes efforts at organizational change vastly different and far more difficult than efforts at change in the private sector.

## Challenges for Leaders

There are many challenges facing modern educational leaders that require time-intensive rethinking about the delivery of instruction and governance structures. These challenges include such time-laden responsibilities as

1. Maintaining organizational legitimacy in the eyes of a skeptical public
2. Exerting curricula vision to raise academic attainment to world-class standards
3. Meeting the needs of culturally diverse and limited-English-speaking students
4. Demonstrating expertise in instructional leadership
5. Managing and resolving conflicts

These responsibilities consume great amounts of time and fiscal resources in the schools; educational leaders also have the problems of student drug abuse, irate parents, legal and legislative mandates, and school violence. Whereas some educational leaders believe that time is a free resource that should be provided by the classroom teachers, in reality time is the most precious of all the resources possessed by teachers. Time simply cannot be given freely by teachers to promote school reform and change. All time investments entail choice, and choice has to reflect personal goals, desired rewards, and possible consequences associated with the lifetime of the teacher.

Two terms in the context of school organizations that will be referred to a great deal throughout this book are organizational *legitimacy* and *visibility*. Organizational legitimacy is the degree to which schools are considered by the community and by parents to be valuable and highly regarded social institutions, that is, community and parental confidence in the schools. Organizational legitimacy typically translates into voter approval of school policies, school bond issues, and tax overrides. Parent participation and support to make the schools a source of pride in the community are also reflective of school organizational legitimacy.

Organizational visibility is the degree to which schools are perceived by the community in comparison to other school organizations such as private schools and other social institutions such as police and fire departments and welfare organizations. The amount of positive and negative press schools receive in the community over issues such as school violence, safety, gangs, and dropout rates affects the school organization's visibility (positive or negative) in that community. *Whereas organizational legitimacy tends to be more objective in nature, school visibility is far more subjective and is a measure of whether and how much the community is aware of the contribution of the schools to the life of the community.* Obviously, there is usually a high association between positive visibility and high legitimacy. There is also a high association between negative visibility and low legitimacy.

School reforms are intended to enhance both positive visibility and high legitimacy. These goals, therefore, should be considered major objectives of the school reform effort. Because time investments by classroom teachers are needed to service the needs of these school reform efforts, the time investments of classroom teachers to the reform effort affect both the visibility and legitimacy of the school organization.

In this and subsequent chapters, *It's About Time* will describe some of the time choice behaviors of classroom teachers and their leaders. These chapters will give specific attention to how the highly significant factor of time manifests itself in the school reform and change process. A multitude of time-sensitive insights and recommendations along with specific leadership strategies for educational leaders will also be presented. Teachers and their school leaders, therefore, should find many of these ideas extremely helpful for understanding the complexity and time sensitivity of the school reform and change process. In short, because school time, teacher time, and school leader time are all interrelated in the school reform and change process, time is the common thread that joins teachers to school organizations and both to the reform and change process.

Classroom teachers and school organizations are vastly different with regard to their time sensitivity, time perceptions, and time investments. This added layer of complexity makes a single magic-bullet approach to time-investment strategies in the school reform and change process illogical and misleading. Instead, what is required is a deeper understanding of how the basic psychosocial marker of time found in classroom teachers affects their behaviors in school organizations, especially regarding their participation in school reform and change efforts.

There are five major time concepts and constructs that will be explored in great detail in this and subsequent chapters:

1. *Time investment:* the ways hours are invested by classroom teachers to attain their personal goals in life. This concept will be referred to as the *time investment portfolio.*

2. *Temporal orientation:* the way classroom teachers orient themselves toward the past, present, and future; also, the way memory and vision produce teacher behaviors in the present. This concept will be referred to as *temporal dominance.*

3. *Sense of time passage:* the way an hour of time is subjectively weighted over the career of a teacher. This subjective weight in time tends to distinguish younger and older teachers in terms of their willingness to participate in the time-consuming activities associated with school reform efforts. This concept will be referred to as the *subjective weighted hour.*

4. *Engagement and participation motivation:* the ratio of benefits or satisfaction derived to the time effort expended. This concept is appropriate for addressing the question, "Is participation worth the time of the classroom teacher?" This participation incentive measure will be referred to as the *satisfaction to time effort ratio,* or S/TE ratio.

5. *Time clock orientation:* the type of overall time patterns that individual teachers and school organizations use to orient and pace their lives. This concept will be referred to as the taxonomy of time clocks consisting of *linear-cyclical and point time.*

The specific objective of this and subsequent chapters, therefore, is to explore how each of these time concepts interacts in the lives of classroom teachers and school organizations engaged in school reform and change. Implications of classroom teacher time sensitivity, time investment, and time perceptions for leadership strategies in an era of time scarcity are then explored.

## Time, Energy, Purpose, and the School Change Process

*Most physical and biological scientists would agree that three of the most important and fundamental forces of change found in nature are time, energy, and purpose.* Purpose in the physical world—the world of nature—might be toward entropy and evolution. When dealing with human nature, purpose is far more of a psychological force, related to lifestyle satisfaction or its components, perceived worth or benefits, fulfillment, and happiness. In essence, these three pillars (time, energy, and purpose) form part of the foundation for understanding the change process in nature as well as in humans and the social organizations they participate in over the course of a lifetime. Time (or its human counterpart, time investment), energy (or its human counterpart, effort), and purpose (or its human counterpart, goals such as lifestyle satisfaction) affect our behaviors every day of our lives because they govern our choices and decision making with regard to time investments. Taken in composite, time, energy, and purpose constitute some of our basic values or motivations toward participation in various types of time-consuming activities in life.

To begin, some general perspectives on time that will tend to limit the discussions and ideas should be noted.

First, when referring to time, it is not a one-dimensional or chronometric view of time that is being examined, but the human behaviors associated with the psychosocial constructs of time such as temporal dominance (past, present, future), and the time investment portfolio or the allocations of time to various types of time-consuming activities over a lifespan.

Second, when referring to U.S. classroom teachers, discussions center mainly on K-12 public school teachers in urban and suburban school district organizations. Of course, many of the same time concepts are appropriate and could be applied to rural and private school K-12 teachers and, to a lesser extent, to college and university teachers.

Because time perceptions and investment affect life processes and behaviors, consider for a moment how these three forces (time, effort, purpose) interact in the following scenarios of teacher behaviors. Special attention should be given to the inclination of teachers to participate in various extra time-consuming activities associated with school organizations.

## Scenario 1

The final bell of the school day rings at a large urban elementary school. One teacher heads straight to the parking lot, gets into a car and drives home or drives to another job (moonlights) in the area, or engages in some other type of time-consuming activity that is not school related. Another teacher stays after school to assist children who need additional help with their schoolwork. For some teachers, participation in after-school activities or volunteering their free time to the school organization simply is not worth their time. It is a question of time, effort, and purpose or the perceived benefits that the time investment represents for the classroom teacher.

## Scenario 2

A bulletin board notice is sent out at a local high school about an after-school meeting on curriculum reform. Unfortunately, only a handful of teachers appear at the meeting. Some teachers believe that the proposed school reform is exactly the type of change that is needed by the school organization. Other teachers remain unconvinced that the proposed reform will help them in the classroom and conclude that the activity is not worth their time. It is a question of time, effort, and purpose or the perceived benefits that the time investment represents for the classroom teacher.

## Scenario 3

A group of teachers attending a faculty meeting are busy grading papers while seemingly oblivious to the presentation being made on the need for school reform and change by the school principal. At precisely 4 p.m. when the meeting is scheduled to conclude, many of the teachers rudely stand up and leave the room. Only a handful of teachers remain to hear the details of the proposed school reform effort. It is a question of time, effort, and purpose or the perceived benefits that the time investment represents for the classroom teacher.

## Scenario 4

One teacher is teaching Algebra I at a local high school. This teacher exhibits the classic symptoms of teacher burnout, that is, a teacher who provides only the minimum amount of time for students in the classroom, uses only easy-to-grade multiple-choice tests, does all grading in class, and never stays after school to assist students. Another Algebra I teacher down the hall exhibits all the characteristics of a committed and caring teacher. This teacher provides more than the minimum amount of time specified for classroom instruction, uses a variety of time-consuming classroom assessment formats that are designed to enhance student learning, takes schoolwork home, and is nearly always available to help students after school. It is a question of time, effort, and purpose or the perceived benefits that the time investment represents for the classroom teacher.

## Scenario 5

Teachers in a rural school district consider themselves to be part of an extended family and integrate their personal, social, and recreational activities around school events. Because the school district is the largest employer in the area and because there are no other competing time-consuming activities in their lives, it is relatively easy to engage teachers in school-related activities. The distinctions between school time and personal time are lessened as all teachers become part of a larger community or "family." Some teachers are attracted to this type of family work environment, whereas other teachers can't wait to leave because they want other types of time-consuming activities in their lives. It is a question of time, effort, and purpose or the perceived benefits that the time investment represents for the classroom teacher.

## Scenario 6

A teacher is asked to participate in a school reform activity related to curriculum. The school organization will provide release time for the teacher by covering the classroom with a substitute teacher. The classroom teacher refuses to participate because the time needed to prepare a substitute teacher lesson plan and the time needed to make up for lost time in the direct instruction of students make participation in reform not worth the added effort. It is a question of time, effort, and purpose or the perceived benefits that the time investment represents for the classroom teacher.

These and countless other stories of teachers and teacher behaviors in school organizations indicate that classroom teachers are an extraordinarily interesting group of individuals to study from the psychosocial perspective of time, effort, and purpose (or perceived benefits). The fact that, in general, teachers age while the children they teach remain the same age can create a serious distortion in the passage of time for many classroom teachers. School organizations require time to reform and change to ensure effective organizational evolution, survival as an institution, and societal legitimacy. Individual teachers require time to attain their goals of lifestyle satisfaction or happiness. In short, the physical world, the world of a classroom teacher, and the world of a school organization can be loosely described in terms of their sense of time, energy, and purpose. As shown in Table 1.1, the clock or the pace of time passage in a teacher's lifetime is linear in orientation (no repetition of time), and the clock for a school organization is cyclical (each year is a repetition of time).

### Time and Human Behavior With Regard to Change

The subject of time, of course, has been intensively examined in the literature of the physical sciences. Much of this literature deals with the precise measurement of time or the one-dimensional,

**TABLE 1.1** A Sense of Time, Energy, and Purpose

|  | The Physical World | A Teacher's World | A School Organization's World |
|---|---|---|---|
| Time clock | Linear and cyclical | Linear | Cyclical |
| Energy | Physical energy input to the process | Physical and mental effort input to the process | Resource input to the process |
| Purpose | Successful evolution as a goal | Lifestyle satisfaction as a goal | Visibility and legitimacy as goals |

quantitative units of time. The accurate measurement of time (seconds, minutes, hours, days, etc.) has had a major influence on human social and organizational development. In fact, if time could not be measured accurately there would be little opportunity for international commerce, and much of the world's business and industry would have to be local time zone based. It was the measurement of time by the use of clocks, more than the steam engine, that was the main catalyst for the industrial revolution. Measuring time to the minute and second across time zones precipitated the rapid expansion of commerce throughout the world. *The accurate measurement of time by means of clocks puts all human beings on a "time" standard of social behavior or a schedule, whether it is a class schedule in a school organization or an airline schedule at an airport.* Once time schedules were designed, the person then had a choice of being a prisoner locked into the time of outside organizations, or a prisoner locked out of the pace of time set by outside organizations.

Time consists of various philosophical, physical, biological, cultural, and psychological components, which, when taken in various combinations, formulate one's personal perception of time. The impact of time and the sense of time passage in life has heavily influence modern art (the works of Dali) and literature (the works of Faulkner) as well as many fields of social science (economics). Psychological, economic, organizational, and sociological time perspectives of behavior have provided the social scientist with fascinating insights regarding the development of humans and the efficiency and effectiveness of their contributions to social organizations.

Time can also have a negative effect on individuals by creating a psychological prison of time scarcity and a sense of time urgency. From an unconscious and psychological perspective, the desire and urge of human beings to escape from the demanding structure or "prison" of time can mainly be found in the psychological literature (Bonaparte, 1940). Discussions and psychological insights with regard to the evolution of time and their impact on social behaviors can be found in the works of Adam (1990), Cottle (1967, 1976), Fraser (1981), and Friedman (1990). The perception of one's time and the impact of temporal dominance (past, present, future) have also been examined in the research literature. The circles test of Cottle (1967, 1976), for example, is of particular interest because it presents a method for ascertaining the temporal dominance in a person or the orientation of the person toward the past, present, and future. "Does the individual teacher act and behave with his or her back toward the future and his or her face toward the past?" or "Does the individual teacher act and behave with his or her face toward the future and his or her back toward the past?" are some of the interesting temporal dominance questions associated with teacher behaviors. The circles test has been successfully used in a wide variety of educational contexts for exploring the behaviors of students, teachers, and youth gangs (Bruno & Maguire, 1993; Smith, 1995). Sociological perspectives for understanding time and its relationship to social behavior in the work organization are of particular interest (Lewis & Weigert, 1981).

Finally, the notion of how time is used as an investment (the consumptive and investment benefits of time) has been explored in economics. Time and its economic implications for the individual has been examined in the research of Sharp (1981) and Leigh (1986). It is this latter perspective combined with the impact of time on human behavior (Douglass & Douglass, 1980; "Time Is Not on Their Side," 1989; Zerubavel, 1981) that is of most interest to the themes presented in this and subsequent chapters of this book.

The extreme importance of time in the school change and reform movement has been recognized by educational research. "Time has become the most limiting resource in the management of the change and reform process" (Purnell & Hill, 1992, p. 19). In another educational research study, "Ask anybody involved in school reform about its most essential ingredient and the answer will most likely be time. Time emerged as the key issues in every analysis of school reform and change appearing in the last decade" (Raywid, 1993, p. 30).

Over the next decade, U.S. public education will see major demographic changes in the composition of its teaching faculties. Tens of thousands of teachers hired in the "golden age" of U.S. education (1960-1975) will retire in the early years of the next decade. These older teachers will be replaced by younger teachers who might, in general, be required to commit more time in their lifetimes to the school organization. To adjust to the anticipated social, economic, and political changes in schooling, the issue of time control will undoubtedly assume key importance for these classroom teachers. Equal to salary and fringe benefits, time control might also become (in some areas it already is) a key issue in collective bargaining negotiations. In short, changes in time and time control of classroom teachers will have a profound effect on the teaching profession and the quality of the lives of teachers.

---

The cost for any school reform or change effort can and should not only be measured in terms of dollars but also, more appropriately, in terms of the resource of time provided by classroom teachers.

---

Presently, there is little doubt that many classroom teachers commit large amounts of their own time to the profession, not only in terms of direct student contact but also after-school and weekend hours of class preparation, grading, paperwork, photocopying, yard duty, meeting with parents, and serving on school committees. Although some teachers commit more than the minimum amount of time needed by the school organization (especially at innovative school sites), other teachers commit only the minimum amounts of time (especially at minimally performing school sites). The cost for any school reform or change effort, therefore, can and should not only be measured in terms of dollars but also, more appropriately, in terms of the resource of time provided by classroom teachers.

## Time and the School Reform Movement

Time is used by classroom teachers for two important purposes: (a) to build their personas as classroom teachers and thus establish their market value to the school organization and (b) to find the personal self in their own psychological journey toward fulfillment and lifestyle satisfaction. Both objectives of teacher time, the persona and the self, can have an important impact on classroom learning because they define the psychological and economic quality of a teacher's life, which in turn affects teaching behavior in the classroom, which in turn affects student learning in the classroom.

Scarcity can be loosely defined as the lack of an important or critical resource that is needed to obtain some a priori defined objective. For both the school organization and classroom teacher, the scarcest and most critical resource of all is time. *For a classroom teacher, it is not time per se that is scarce, but an overcommitment of time to a certain role in life that creates a situation requiring time.* The greater the number of temporally embedded events in a classroom teacher's life that have to be addressed between two points in physical time, for example, additional required units of curriculum to be taught between the beginning and end of the semester, the shorter is the perceived temporal distance between these points. It is the perceived shortened distance between these points in time that leaves the teacher with a sense of time scarcity. Adding a weekly IEP meeting, a school site council meeting, and sponsorship of the senior class are the types of events in a teacher's life that can lead to the sense of time scarcity.

School reform essentially requires that teachers readjust and sometimes radically change their time-based behaviors, attitudes, skills, knowledge, philosophies, and routines that have been built and refined over a long career in the classroom. The major challenge for educational leadership in an era of time scarcity, therefore, is to create conditions and incentives for classroom teachers to make those needed time changes and readjustments.

The rationale for making educational leadership more aware of time in the lifetime of a teacher is that the quality of life of a teacher is as important to classroom learning as the school curricula or any school reform effort. An unhappy, burned-out, dropout teacher can be far more harmful to classroom learning than some of the possible imperfections in instructional delivery that the school reform effort is attempting to address. The quality of life of classroom teachers is dictated, in part, by the degree to which teachers have a sense of control over their time investments in their lifetimes and the way time has been invested in their lifetimes.

Unlike school organizations, teachers use their time in a lifetime primarily to attain what might best be described as lifestyle satisfaction, happiness, individuation, self-actualization, or whatever branch of psychological thought that the teacher subscribes to in life. In essence, the "purpose" of time is to purchase personal happiness—whether happiness through the profession or outside of the profession. With the virtual monopoly of school organizations to deliver educational services, with a provision of job security via tenure for its member teachers, and with the repetitive cyclical nature of the instructional program, time plays a completely different role in school organizations than it does in other social and private work organizations. Hence, what we know about time and its association with change, productivity, legitimacy, job satisfaction, and so forth in private corporations is not too relevant to school organizations. *The time uniqueness of both the teaching profession and the school organization, therefore, severely limits any possible insights that might have been developed by research on time in the private sector.*

Naturally, the context and type of school organization, that is, charter school, rural school, urban school, magnet school, university school, or innovative school, along with the professional climate of the school regarding peer pressure from other teachers, can also have a great deal of impact on teachers' views of time and their participation in extra time-consuming activities. In certain competitive and "market-driven" reform-minded school contexts, where the selection of teachers is under strong school site control, time commitment is expected. In many situations, teachers "let go" from these types of market-driven school organizations are placed at other nearby schools in the school district. These noncompetitive and non-market-driven schools typically don't have any specific personnel policies with regard to teachers' extra time investments for reform and change. Teachers at these school sites, therefore, have less incentive to invest any of their extra time in the school organization. All else being equal, the gain at one school site in terms of additional time investment by teachers might be offset by the loss of time investment by teachers at another nearby school site.

When comparing time investments of teachers in school organizations with time investments of professionals in private sector organizations, several interesting differences emerge.

In the private sector, the professional staff has to assume a "free agency" type of status in the organization. After making the needed large initial time investments in their early careers (where they are essentially underpaid for their efforts), many of these professionals are terminated by the organization in the latter parts of their career when they are less willing to make the needed time investment. Termination in midcareer, when these employees can't make the needed time investments and are slightly overpaid (called downsizing), unfortunately is now commonplace in many private organizations. The free agency mentality of the professional staff tends to devalue organizational loyalty and institutional memory.

Although the free agency of professional employees in the private sector might be appropriate for some high-tech industries, it is totally inappropriate for public school organizations. Whereas reform and change in these private industries have been typically based on massive layoffs and employee downsizing, public school organizations have generally been immune from the downsizing practice. Classroom teachers simply cannot be made into free agents where they have to hunt for teaching positions every 5 or 10 years. There is intrinsic educational value for students in having instructional continuity, teacher loyalty, tradition, and institutional memory. A far better approach to reform and change is to appreciate the multitude of problems, mainly centered on the time needs of classroom teachers, and then adjust or engineer school reforms accordingly within the time frameworks of the classroom teacher.

With this premise in mind, this book is not about school reform and the time management of teachers, but the more complex, and potentially more powerful, subject of the *lifetime management* of classroom teachers. If reform and change in school organizations are for the long haul, then appreciating teachers' lifetime management becomes an important leadership principle.

> Time management = More time in the day
> Lifetime management = More life into the time

## Summary

The massive problems facing school organizations in the future will require significant amounts of reform and change. These change efforts will have to include replacing outdated curriculums; ensuring that ethnic and cultural diversity is accepted; detracking classrooms; adding new technology; meeting the needs of Goals 2000; including students with special needs in mainstream classes; acknowledging pressure to provide drug and AIDS education and developing curriculums to solve society's other problems; and developing site-based decision making, new instructional strategies, constructivism, and interdisciplinary instruction. Each of these proposed school reforms and changes can only be accomplished if classroom teachers are willing to give the time for planning meetings, committee meetings, curriculum writing meetings, professional development, and so on. The increased demand for teacher time will thus become an expectation for the lifelong career as a classroom teacher. Because the change and reform process will be ongoing and constant, teachers will have to adjust their time clocks for a long-term career in the classroom. In a constructivist classroom, last year's lesson plans simply won't work, because instruction and learning will have to be based on the needs of *this* child in *this* year. To successfully implement the needed school reforms and changes, school organizations need the experience, wisdom, and vision of all classroom teachers—new as well as experienced. *The challenge for educational leaders in an era of time scarcity, then, is to find time-sensitive ways to draw all teachers—young and old— to participate in the reform process.*

In this chapter, time, energy, and purpose have been described as the three forces that control the change processes in the universe. These three fundamental forces also have relevance for school leaders concerned about teacher participation in the school reform process. Time, effort, and lifestyle satisfaction are comparable to time, energy, and purpose and provide important management principles on which to understand the behaviors of classroom teachers involved in the reform and change process.

Finally, during times of school organizational transition, change, and reform, the loudest and most vocal complaint by classroom teachers is quite logically over the school reform's infringement on their personal time. Time needed for reform and change in school organizations is time that is drawn from the finite amount of time available in the lifetime of a teacher. The most important question in the mind of a classroom teacher, therefore, is if the compensation associated with the school reform effort is worth the added time effort needed. To convince teachers of the need to provide the extra time to participate, the burden of proof is with the leadership of school organizations. Thus, time, effort, and purpose (or perceived satisfaction and benefits) all become important components of an individual teacher's decision to participate in the extra time-consuming activities associated with school reform and change.

## Perspectives, Points of View, Discussion

- How would you describe some of the important differences between time management and lifetime management with regard to the behaviors of classroom teachers?
- Should time be considered as an input, output, or process in terms of school reform and change efforts?
- In your professional experience, have you ever noticed any time differences (perception, investment, and sensitivity) between teachers by gender, age, subject matter taught, and level of instruction?
- In addition to time, are there other important factors or core human values that have impeded the progress of school reform in the school organization? Can these factors be indirectly related to time perception?
- Is the concept "time is money" of equal importance in the context of school reform and in the context of the lifetime of a classroom teacher?
- How does the teaching profession differ from other professions with regard to time sensitivity, time perceptions, and time investment?

# 2

# Defining the Self With Time

*You are in the worst possible job because you never have time.*

GEORGE ELIOT

- The Pace of Time in School and Life: Time, Clocks, and Time Orientation
- Psychosocial Components of Time and Classroom Teacher Behavior
- The Time Relationship Among Memory, Vision, and Behavior of Teachers
- Investments of Time and Teacher Behavior
- Summary
- Perspectives, Points of View, Discussion

## The Pace of Time in School and Life: Time, Clocks, and Time Orientation

There are many psychosocial factors that affect human behavior, such as motivation, personality, and aptitudes. Many of these factors, however, have embedded in their construct a temporal or time sensitivity, time perception, and a time investment type of preference. Type A and Type B personalities, for example, have differing views on the value of time. Aptitude is usually referred to as the ability to accomplish a set of tasks at a high level of quality in a short or fixed amount of time. Why we should study time in the context of school organizational change and reform, therefore, has important applied as well as theoretical justifications. The perception, sensitivity, and investment of time can be considered as a foundation trait of a personality or a trait that can affect all other traits. In the school organizational change and reform process, time is important to study because it affects teachers' behavior in the classroom and their willingness to participate in the "extra" time-consuming change and reform activities of the school organizations. Time also affects the delivery of the school reform effort, as designed by educational leaders, to the classroom.

In addition, the psychosocial construct of time is important to study in the context of teachers in school organizations for the following reasons:

1. Time is a fundamental currency of exchange (things don't cost money, they cost time) between teachers and school organizations.
2. Time links the past to the present to the future in the school organization.
3. Time is needed by classroom teachers to develop their personas as educators, that is, classroom teachers, subject matter specialists, school administrators.
4. Time is needed by classroom teachers to find the self or lifestyle happiness and satisfaction in life. Teachers use their time investments to seek fulfillment in life.
5. Time is related to information-seeking behaviors that are associated with the school reform and change process.

The first chapter discussed the importance of increasing the awareness of educational leaders toward the concept of time in the lifetime of a teacher and the importance of time in the evolution of school organizations. Special emphasis in Chapter 1 was given to the notion that time, effort, and lifestyle satisfaction (time, energy, and purpose) are fundamental forces that affect how the change and reform process in the school organization is managed.

**TABLE 2.1** Taxonomies of Time, Clocks, and Temporal Orientation

| | |
|---|---|
| Linear-cyclical-point time | The sense of beginnings, ends, cycles, etc., or the clock that paces human behavior |
| Physiological time | The feel or subjective sense of time passage with aging |
| Physical time | The actual hour, year, minute |
| Psychological time | An individual's orientation toward the past, present, and future |

This chapter extends and examines some of these time concepts with specific reference to taxonomies that measure the passage of time and the components of time that affect the behaviors of classroom teachers.

First, there are the various taxonomies and orientations toward time or the way in which individuals are "paced" by the clock (see Table 2.1).

## Psychosocial Components of Time and Classroom Teacher Behavior

### *Linear, Cyclical, Point Time*

The passage of time over a lifetime can be viewed in three different forms: a linear time frame perspective, a cyclical time frame perspective, and a point time frame perspective (see Table 2.2). The cyclical and linear perspective of time have particular relevance to the classroom teacher because they tend to come into direct conflict in the school organization. A linear time frame (a set beginning, a set end, and a set interval such as birth and death) is most characteristic of private sector work organizations and all human beings. Point time is time of the moment and has little relevance to the school reform process or classroom teacher behaviors other than random events at school such as violence, vandalism, or other "one-time" events.

School organizations, unlike most private sector work organizations, are best characterized by a cyclical view of time (no set beginning, no set end—but a set interval). Similar to cycles of the moon,

**TABLE 2.2** Linear Versus Cyclical Versus Point Time
            Characteristics

| | |
|---|---|
| Linear time | The aging process—birth, life, death—time that has a set beginning and a set end with no interval defined (the hourglass clock) |
| Cyclical time | The organizational process—each year nearly the same activities are repeated—no set beginning—no set end—interval defined—repetition of cycles (the face watch) |
| Moment, point, or accounting unit time | The free agent, MBA, or lawyer billing type of time—no set beginning—no set end—no defined interval (the digital watch); not common in school organizations) |

the school organization has the same grade levels repeated and sequences or lessons taught at each cycle for each year. For example, Algebra I essentially repeats itself each year, the senior prom repeats itself each year, the football team repeats itself each year, and each grade level repeats itself each year. For a fifth-grade teacher, the students remain exactly the same age and thus repeat themselves each year ostensibly over the entire lifetime of the teacher's career. Time reference for teachers, looking at the school organization, therefore, has a cyclical time frame due to its repetitiveness. Cyclical time gives one a sense of psychological security. Events repeat themselves over time and thus provide teachers with an opportunity to develop familiarity and fluency in activities that are needed by the school organization. Teachers who entered the teaching profession because of this unique cyclical time frame characteristic might experience massive psychological problems or insecurity when adjusting to school organizations that are moving toward a more linear time frame or market-driven (charter schools, magnet schools) orientation. Thus, a major change in the work environment for classroom teachers in the future would be for school organizations to move toward a linear time perspective.

The linear time clock of the classroom teacher and the cyclical time clock of the school organization can sometimes create conflict over needed time investments of classroom teachers. While the teacher is delivering instruction on a cyclical time clock, the teacher

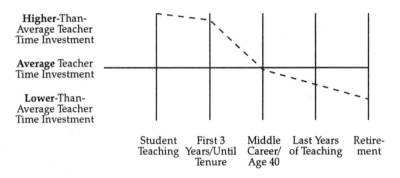

**Figure 2.1.** Hypothetical Time Investment Over a Career as a Classroom Teacher

is, of course, aging on a linear time clock. This duality can become a major source of conflict for ensuring teacher participation in school reform and change efforts.

In a recently released film, *Mr. Holland's Opus,* much was revealed about the cyclical-linear time clock conflict between the school organization and the classroom teacher. The film's main character, Mr. Holland, tells a fellow teacher that he entered the teaching profession so that he could have the time to write his symphony. In disbelief, the colleague informs Mr. Holland that he has been in the profession for 10 years and never has any free time. A dynamic framework is then described with regard to the time to establish the persona of the teacher (of music) and time to find the self of the teacher (a music composer). Time investments that teachers are willing to make to the profession of teaching along with the age of the teacher might generate a graph similar to that presented in Figure 2.1.

Given the cyclical time frame perspective of the school organization and the linear time frame perspective of the individual classroom teacher, it is understandable that many teachers tend to make large time investments, or front-load, their time investments in their early careers (when they feel that they have few time-competing activities), then capitalize on these early time investments by making less of a time investment in their later careers (when they feel that they have many time-competing activities). The major difference in time frame perspective between school organizations and private sector organizations, however, is that in the private sector, individuals have to continually invest and reinvest in a career to even have a job or to be able to "sell" their time to the organization at the market clearing price. In the private sector, both the organization and the individual professional operate under the same linear time frame clock.

Because tenure essentially guarantees job security for the classroom teacher regardless of extra time investments made to the school organization, there is little job protection incentive to reinvest time in a teaching career. The nature of a cyclical time frame in the school organization is that the same time investment made in early-career time efficiency has a return each year provided that the classroom teacher is teaching the same subject matter or course. Teachers become attached to the familiar pedagogical routines, and with their isolation in the classroom from other teachers they develop a set teaching routine requiring minimal additional time investment. In short, the teacher gets the job down (fluency) or has an opportunity to reduce time effort over the career because teaching tasks are repeated each year.

Although the private sector is rapidly moving toward a free agency type of employee (no loyalty but front-loaded time investments and dismissal toward midcareer), the school organization, due to teacher tenure laws, has to accommodate the time needs of teachers over their entire career in the classroom. Younger teachers who are now front-loading their time investments in their teaching careers might exhibit similar behaviors as the older teachers in the school organization (see Table 2.3). This phenomenon of time investment propensity is not so much related to the age of the teacher but rather to the unique cyclical time structure of the school organization. One should not, therefore, blame older teachers for creating impediments to school reform and change. The nature of the aging process and associated time investments over a teacher's lifetime make the behavior of optimal time investments rather than maximum time investments understandable from an economic and psychological perspective.

Here are some fairly typical classroom teacher scenarios regarding time, time investments, and teacher behaviors.

### Early-Career Teachers

Some graduate students, on contemplating what to do with their lives, go into the teaching profession so that they can have the

**TABLE 2.3** Time Investment Portfolio Shifts With Age

| Age of Teacher | Objective Purpose of Time Investments | Time Investment |
|---|---|---|
| 20-34 | Career building | Major investments in selling-time activities (outside organizations) |
| 35-49 | Career integration | Major investments in giving-time activities (family and friends) |
| 50-65 | Safe landing after career | Major investments in spending-time activities (hobbies and interests) |

time to do what they really want to do, for example, be a filmmaker, a writer, a composer, a real estate developer. Other graduates go into the profession for other time-laden reasons such as summer vacations, 3:00 dismissals, frequent vacations, and so forth. Because the pecuniary benefits of beginning teaching are low, one must assume that the nonpecuniary benefits of teaching such as time control are of extreme importance for students interested in pursuing a teaching career. The classroom reality for these individuals is that teaching becomes a far more time-intensive career than they expected, and many drop out or burn out of the profession. Many of these beginning teachers support school reforms that are consistent with their professional goals, but most are neutral or "go with the flow," because their past time investments in classroom teaching are low.

### Midcareer Teachers

A middle-aged teacher having conflicts and competing time-consuming interests in life starts experiencing burnout and the beginnings of a midlife crisis. These mature teachers simply can't find the needed time that the profession demands, and even though they might love teaching, the teaching act itself requires too much of their time and effort. In a competition with other time-consuming activities in their lives such as health, families, and relationships, time-consuming school reform activities tend to take a back seat. Many of these teachers have high time investments in their past teaching practices and actively oppose any proposed school reform that will increase their time effort in the classroom. They already have teaching "down," so the reform is considered to be not worth their added time effort.

## Veteran or Older Teachers

Older classroom teachers who are nearing retirement after a long career in teaching begin to invest time in the self. These time-consuming activities include spending time on hobbies and personal interests. In essence, many of these teachers would rather go to meetings on early retirement, or on their hobbies, than on revising school curricula. These teachers are already planning for what they really want to do with their remaining time in life. Some of these teachers are indifferent and don't even bother about or ignore school reform or change efforts because they are looking forward to getting out of the school organization. Others are not motivated to participate in school reform efforts because they will not be teaching long enough to reap any of the benefits of their participation.

## Valuing Time

The terms *individuation, satisfaction,* and *self-actualization* are drawn from different branches of psychology and reflect a basic human goal of wanting to find happiness in a given lifetime. For most individuals, in the first half of life, time is used to define the persona to others in society and, in the second half of life, time is used to find the personal self. The important journey of the search for happiness and fulfillment in life is purchased with time drawn from a lifetime. Material objects in a society—such as cars, a home, computers—have a "cost" in terms of time units from a lifetime. Different types of teaching personas, in time units, also have a cost.

Because classroom teachers use time to define their personas as educators and to define the self, time in the lifetime of a teacher is contextual and dynamic. *It is highly likely, given certain demographic characteristics of the teaching staff, that at a particular school there would be two groups of teachers—those who are at a stage in life where they are defining their personas as teaching professionals and those who are at a stage in life where they are trying to find their selves.* This dichotomy over the use of time for the development of the persona (usually younger teachers) and the use of time for the development of the self (usually older teachers) presents unusual and complex challenges for educational leaders in the school organization.

Adding to the notion of time needed to define the persona and time needed to define the self is the important relationship between the value of the self (self-esteem) and the way time is economically valued by a society. The value of people's time in a free marketplace is an indirect measure of their value or worth in society. Organizations, by paying for or purchasing the time in the lifetime of a teacher, are indirectly placing a value or establishing the worth of the classroom teacher. Paying teachers as if their time is not worth (economically) very much can thus have a devastating impact on teachers' self-esteem: It undervalues their personas and their selves. Adding insult to injury would be a situation where the school organization would be both underpaying teachers for their time and requiring more free time from them to serve the needs of school reform.

An important point, therefore, can be made that if school organizations do not economically compensate (pecuniary benefit) their teachers, and do not compensate their teachers in either social relationships or professional development, these teachers will find places where their time is worth more to the development of the self. If there is an economic need for a teacher to moonlight, there is ample opportunity for teachers to do so. Moonlighting activities provide teachers with external material, social, or personal compensation for their "extra" time. For these teachers, time is simply withdrawn from the school organization and invested elsewhere, because the self of the teacher requires some form of reaffirmation of the worth for one's time, whether economic, social, or personal interest. Teachers, being intelligent and well educated, will tend to seek this time worth either in or outside of the school organization. If teachers don't find time worth in school activities, they will look outside of school to find activities that are worth their time. For these reasons, a quality or high-time-worth lifetime for a classroom teacher (material, social, personal development compensation) is far more efficacious and logical for improving student learning than a school reform effort that is directed at learning and has to be serviced by unhappy, low-time-worth teachers.

## Physiological Time and the Aging of a Classroom Teacher

Finally, there is the important psychological time concept that is associated with the sense of time passage or the "feel" of time. This concept is referred to as the subjective weighted hour. As a teacher ages in life, the perceived worth of an additional hour of time investment changes. The hour itself has a different subjective sense or feel for a 25-year-old teacher than it does for a 50-year-old teacher. This concept will be explored in greater detail in later chapters, but it is based on the unconscious realization of the ratio of time in hours lived in life to time in hours remaining in life. For example, a 50-year-old teacher's hour is weighted of more value than a 20-year-old teacher's because time is perceived as being scarcer.

> The worth of each additional hour of time investment demanded by the school organization is extraordinarily different for different-aged teachers.

Because of the subjective weighted hour concept, the professional and psychological worth of each additional hour of time investment demanded by the school organization is extraordinarily different for different-aged teachers. For educational leaders in school organizations with large numbers of older teachers, the subjective weighted hour becomes particularly problematic with regard to school reform and change and ensuring the teachers' participation in reform.

Physiological time, or age time, is an important concept for educational leadership to appreciate, because the needed time effort ($TE$) or energy needed to perform an activity also tends to increase. As teachers age, physical impairments and observed behaviors such as a lessened vitality, depression, impatience, lack of endurance, poorer eyesight, and poorer hearing might affect classroom and organizational performance. By increasing $TE$ and lowering satisfaction ($S$) associated with a given task, activities that used to be pleasurable, or have high $S$ to $TE$ ratios, early in the career now have low $S/TE$ ratios later in the career.

## The Time Relationship Among
## Memory, Vision, and Behavior of Teachers

Temporal dominance (see Table 2.4) or orientation toward the past, present, or future can also affect classroom teacher behavior. For the sake of clarity, past, present, and future linked through time can be viewed as follows:

*Past (memory or experience):* provides the mental and conceptual structures for present behavior. The past provides the template for decision making that is based on traditions, experiences, and actions. The choices in the present, therefore, are based on (a) the types and quality of time investments in the past, (b) the amount or extent of these time investments, (c) the benefits or satisfactions derived from these time investments (investment and consumptive benefits), and (d) the random traumatic experience or occurrence that limits present options. The past thus forms the philosophy or decision-making structure for an individual in the present.

*Present (reality):* the physical reality that is the "now" of a lifetime. The present is limited by the actions and time investments made by the individual in the past. Future vision is also connected to events in the time-consuming events in the present. There is no luck or a lottery, only preparation (time investments) that meets opportunity (vision).

*Future (vision and expectations):* the mental and conceptual structure for expectations and hopes in life. The goal is lifestyle satisfaction, self-actualization, and happiness. Random probabilities of events happening in life are transformed to realistic possibilities by time investment in the present. Fatalism or determinism (external locus of control) attempts to avoid the need for vision of a future (in the hands of God or luck). For most classroom teachers, success and self-esteem are tied to accomplishing a personal vision for a future. The future presents conceptual structures for decision making in the present, whereas the past offers the conceptual structure for available choices or possibilities in the present. Some visions are realistic (leading to happiness and self-esteem) and some visions are unrealistic (leading to frustration and despair).

**TABLE 2.4** Time Orientation and Related Temporal Behaviors

| | |
|---|---|
| Temporal dominance | Vision of past, present, and future events in life—provides memory—control of behavior and vision for a future (lives for the future—lives in the past) |
| Time investments | Actual investments in time by teachers to maximize some lifestyle satisfaction objective (time for family, work, recreation, and relaxation) |

Temporal dominance attempts to establish the time relationship among past (memory), present (behavior), and future (vision) for classroom teachers. Many cultures have proverbs similar to the following: "To live in the past is to ignore the present; to ignore the past is to threaten the future." Some classroom teachers concentrate on the way education and students used to be and ignore the future in their teaching practices. These are teachers with their faces toward the past and their backs to the future who have no idea that children have changed over the years. Other classroom teachers only have vision for a future in education and basically dismiss or ignore past educational experiences. These are teachers with their faces toward the future and their backs to the past who repeat many of the same mistakes of the past. *The behaviors of classroom teachers in school organizations are often reflective of their temporal dominance and thus provide a clue into the type of behavior they will exhibit in the classroom.* More important, the attitudes of these classroom teachers toward school reform and change are also a reflection of their temporal dominance. Both types of teachers, memory dominant and vision dominant, can function in the school organization. The ideal situation is to have both memory and vision with regard to teaching practices and to have school reform based on past successes and failures as much as future visions.

The relationship among memory (past), behavior (present), and vision (future) for teachers is closely associated with the types of professional experiences or personal crises (both positive and negative) they have experienced in the classroom. The professional or personal crisis in the past forms part of the character or identity of the teacher in the school organization and thus affects that teacher's professional behavior in the present and vision for himself or herself in the future.

Teachers who achieve their identity as a classroom teacher without any sort of past professional or personal crisis tend to stress the future more than the present or past. These classroom teachers have strong vision for their career, but little memory. Teachers who have no sense of identity as a classroom teacher tend to emphasize their present and ignore the future as an educator and past educational traditions. Teachers who achieve identity as a classroom teacher through some form of professional or personal crisis usually have a more balanced sense of time between past, present, and future. They don't ignore the past, nor do they live in it. They nicely combine vision and memory to affect their present classroom behavior.

---

If neither memory nor vision are present in a classroom teacher, then the school organization can find itself at extreme risk of school reform failure because there will be no guideline or framework for behavior.

---

School reform and change activities that are composed of teachers who have a poor sense of what preceded them (no tradition and no memory) and teachers with no vision (no sense of the future) have no temporal anchor to their professional classroom behavior. Staff development and training in school organizations engaged in reform, therefore, should incorporate teachers with both memory (generally older teachers) and vision (generally younger teachers).

For a classroom teacher, the time relationship between past, present, and future in life is analogous to a chess game. In life, one positions one's self with past moves, makes a present move to avoid checkmate (failure or unhappiness), and so on. Physical drives, norms, competition, and psychological needs all affect the personal decision-making process with regard to making these moves. To do well in life, as in chess, one needs to know the rules that govern the game, the consequences of certain moves, and how to make the best of poor positions. Sometimes random and unexpected traumatic events occur in a teacher's lifetime that affect his or her position or options in life (sickness, death of loved ones, other calamities, bad teaching experience, etc.). Choices still have to be made and adjusted accordingly to stay involved with teaching and life. Sometimes teachers give up or capitulate and do not make any choice and essentially "do their time." Yet the "game" has to run its course to retirement. Sometimes teachers hope to change the rules of the game in their favor through changes in school policies. In any case, for classroom teachers, the past (experience that yields options in the present) and the future (visions that require decisions in the present) are strongly related to the present through time.

In a school organization, memory and vision are similar to the engines of a two-engine plane. Both engines would be needed for a smooth flight. Although one could be successful using only one engine (focus only on the past, focus only on the future), the ride might not be too smooth. Eliminating older teachers from the reform and change process, by pushing them out because of excessive time demands or otherwise marginalizing their contributions to the school organization, can only be detrimental to school reform efforts. It is far better to understand older teachers' time needs and then capitalize on their memory than to marginalize them or push them out of the organizational reform and change process by ignoring their time needs.

By examining personal, family, societal, and school organizational (work) perceptions and orientations toward the past, present, and future, implications can be drawn for understanding classroom teacher behavior in the school organization (see Table 2.5).

## Investments of Time and Teacher Behavior

The time investment portfolio of a classroom teacher refers to the types of time investments that are made among various competing time-consuming activities in a lifetime.

Bruno (1995) has applied the concept of a time investment portfolio to at-risk and normal-attaining high school students. The time allocation preferences of teachers also have been reported (Stark, Lowther, & Austin, 1985). The objective or purpose of these time investments is to increase lifestyle satisfaction; that is, these time investments attempt to define the persona of the teacher to others and also to find the personal self. There are essentially four types of time-consuming activities in a time investment portfolio. All of these

**TABLE 2.5**  Time Relationship Between Past, Present, and Future
              for Classroom Teachers

| Temporal Dominance | Individuals, Family, and Society | School Organizations |
|---|---|---|
| Past | **Personal orientation**<br>Memory | **Work orientation**<br>Standard operating<br>procedures |
| | **Family orientation**<br>Family photo album,<br>diaries, heirlooms | Yearbooks<br>Traditions<br>Loyalty<br>Trust |
| | **Societal orientation**<br>Museums, libraries<br>Culture, history<br>Religious organizations<br>Military | Rules<br>Credentials<br>Expertise<br>Experience |
| Present | **Personal orientation**<br>Behavior—the "now"<br>Preparation for future | **Work orientation**<br>Control<br>Class schedules<br>Schedules |
| | **Family orientation**<br>"Taking care of business"<br>"Making ends meet" | Curriculum<br>Meetings<br>Faculty meetings |
| | **Societal orientation**<br>Balancing the budget<br>Maintaining society<br>and infrastructure | |
| Future | **Personal orientation**<br>Vision<br>An unopened present<br>Human capital formation<br>and investment | **Work orientation**<br>Change<br>Technology<br>School reform<br>Facilities<br>Planning |
| | **Family orientation**<br>Expectations and<br>financial investment | New curriculums<br>New facilities |
| | **Societal orientation**<br>Social planning and<br>investment | |

time investments relate to the directedness or benefits associated with the time investment.

Here are the definitions of the four main classifications of time investments of classroom teachers (see also Table 2.6).

*Type I, or outer-directed time: The organization-centered teacher* is affected by the need to compete in society and earn a living. Teachers allocate their limited time in their lifetime to achieving outer-world goals of material attainment, money, position, status, power. Outer-directed time investment teachers have as an objective the desire to "sell" their time to the school organization.

The outer-directed, "selling time" type of teacher could be a workaholic (have a career in school administration as an objective) or have a higher propensity to moonlight outside of the school organization. Outer-directed teachers can become great proponents for school reform and change if they are convinced it will help them attain their material goals.

*Type II, or other-directed time: The student-centered teacher* "gives" time to others to build friendships and relationships in life. This type of time investment is defined by the psychological need of an individual for love and approval of others. Teachers who are other directed value the school and student and teacher friendships they have nurtured over years of working at the same school site. These teachers look for acceptance by their peers, loyalty, and friendships.

Other-directed teachers can become great advocates of school reform and change if they are convinced it will help students and help build meaningful relationships in life.

*Type III, or inner-directed time: The self-centered teacher* has a personal need for development and creativity. The inner-directed teacher strives for and "spends" time on creative expression and personal development whether it be in the arts, hobbies, or recreation. Time is very precious to inner-directed teachers because they are oriented toward a personal use of time and are busy with their own interests, hobbies, and pursuits.

Inner-directed teachers can become great advocates of school reform and change if they are convinced of its creativity, if they have a creative contribution, and/or if there is some free time made available for them to pursue the other things they really want in life.

**TABLE 2.6** Time Investment Orientations of Teachers

| | |
|---|---|
| Organization centered | Outer directed—"selling" time ("Time is money"—British proverb) |
| Student centered | Other directed—"giving" time ("Time not spent on love is time wasted"—Italian proverb) |
| Self-centered | Inner directed—"spending" time ("Time is a stream where I go fishing"—Thoreau) |
| Noncentered | Nondirected—"killing" time ("Just do it"®—Popular Nike commercial) |

*Type IV, or nondirected time: The noncentered teacher* is rare in school organizations because for these individuals, time investments are based on the notion of passing, filling, or killing time.

Nondirected teachers in a school organization are usually given poor evaluations by their school administrator. Because these teachers consider their time at school to be a "filler," they are not interested in school reform or change, and very little can be done to involve them in school reform or change activities.

In a school organization, the observable classroom teacher types or professional teaching personas are nicely aligned to these time investment portfolios (see Table 2.7).

Using the framework of a time investment portfolio, the investment of time of a classroom teacher becomes primarily an economic or "maximize benefit" type of time investment decision. These benefits of time can either be investment benefits (material, social, personal development) or consumptive benefits (entertainment).

Naturally, overlaid on top of time investments are both linear and cyclical time frame perceptions of teachers in the school organization (see Table 2.8).

A final element in understanding the nature of the individual time investment portfolio, or purpose of time, is to appreciate the dynamic quality of time over the lifetime of a teacher. "Is an activity worth my time?" becomes an important question that has to be resolved

**TABLE 2.7** Time Investments and Teacher Types

| | |
|---|---|
| Organization centered | Outer-directed teachers: Lifestyle objectives are oriented toward material accomplishment; seek higher salary, moonlighting, pursue higher education degrees. |
| Student centered | Other-directed teachers: Lifestyle objectives are oriented toward maintaining and developing relationships; seek friendships in social organizations such as volunteer organizations and church groups outside of the school organization. |
| Self-centered | Inner-directed teachers: Lifestyle objectives are oriented toward personal development and accomplishment; seek personal development, hobbies, special interests, and recreation. |
| Noncentered | Nondirected teachers: Lifestyle objectives are oriented toward entertainment and filling time; seek pursuits to be entertained in life or to fill time. |

for each teacher at each stage of life and at each stage of a teaching career. The satisfaction to time effort ($S/TE$) ratio is, therefore, used as an indirect measure of the attractiveness of the time-consuming activity. Educational leaders, in an era of time scarcity, attempt to address the question of worth to $TE$ by examining participation rates of teachers in the time-consuming activities of the school organization. Ideally, educational leaders should attempt to raise $S$ to higher levels and reduce $TE$ to lower levels for a school reform activity to attract teachers to participate with their extra time. For example, feeding teachers with a high-quality meal at a school reform meeting is one method of raising $S$, and providing e-mail summaries and an abstract of events are methods of reducing $TE$. The $S/TE$ ratios associated with school reform activities will be explored in subsequent chapters.

**TABLE 2.8** A Taxonomy of Time in School Settings

| Time Type | Time Directedness | School Time |
|---|---|---|
| **Linear time** (Nonrecurring time-consuming activities such as aging) | **"Selling" time** (Time to build equity and human capital) | Work on a new credential |
| | **"Giving" time** (Time to establish a relationship) | Staying after school to help students |
| | **"Spending" time** (Time to develop talents and interests) | Developing a new course based on your interests |
| | **"Filling" time** (Watching TV; entertainment) | Instructional down time; free period; recovery |
| **Cyclical time** (Recurring time-consuming activities such as anniversaries and holidays) | **"Selling" time** (Time for repetitive work organization assignments) | Teaching the same class each year |
| | **"Giving" time** (Time to maintain relationships) | Keeping in touch with former students |
| | **"Spending" time** (Time to prepare for special events or maintain interests and hobbies) | Coordinate homecoming activities; design program |
| | **"Filling" time** (Time for sleep) | |

## Summary

Understanding the role of time in the context of the lifetime of a teacher is fundamental to understanding and developing more effective strategies to increase teacher participation in school reform. This leadership challenge is especially acute for ensuring the participation of older teachers in the school organization.

This chapter discussed the important role of physical, psychological, and physiological time, and linear and cyclical time frame perspectives, as a prerequisite for understanding teacher behavior in school organizations. Specific time-oriented concepts such as temporal dominance (past, present, future) or memory, vision, and behavior were also examined. Finally, time investment portfolios (selling, giving, spending, and passing time) of classroom teachers were defined to the degree to which they provide a blueprint or marker for the behaviors of classroom teachers. This latter notion of a time investment portfolio can be important in providing policy-related insight for educational leaders attempting to increase teacher participation in the school reform and change process. Finally, the satisfaction $(S)$ or expected compensation (monetary, social, or personal) to time effort $(TE)$ ratio was presented as a useful marker for educational leaders to understand teacher behavior in school organizations.

Because time is needed by classroom teachers to earn a living, develop relationships, and develop themselves, questions regarding teacher participation in reform and change over the career of the classroom teacher are fundamentally a matter of time. In short, school reform and change is fundamentally about time, and the cost for school reform is not about dollars but about extra time taken from the lifetimes of teachers.

## Perspectives, Points of View, Discussion

- How does time serve as a bridge between past, present, and future in the context of the school change and reform process?
- Do you think there is a link between time investment and personal happiness or life fulfillment in classroom teachers?
- How does vision for a future by a classroom teacher affect his or her time investments with regard to school reform?
- How do linear time frame and cyclical "clock" time frame relate to the school reform movement and the lives of classroom teachers?
- Do you think there is a different "feel" for time as classroom teachers age in their careers?

# 3

# Time in the Lifetimes of Teachers

*Time is life's greatest teacher; unfortunately, it kills all its pupils.*

HECTOR BERLIOZ (1803-1869)

---

- Time and the Search for Lifestyle Satisfaction
- Time and Earning a Living as a Teacher
- Time and the Personas of Classroom Teachers
- Teachers at Midlife: Changes in the Sense of Time Passage Over a Teaching Career
- Summary
- Perspectives, Points of View, Discussion

---

## Time and the Search for Lifestyle Satisfaction

---

In the first half of a lifetime, time is used to build the persona as a classroom teacher. In the second half of a lifetime, time is used by classroom teachers to find the "self."

---

Who are these people we call classroom teachers? Do they really have lives outside of the classroom? Do they have material wants and desires like other professionals in the workforce?

Should society view teachers as missionaries with unlimited time and teaching more as a vocation receiving psychological compensation? Should classroom teachers be viewed by educational leaders as having the idealism of a Mother Teresa and be expected to give their "extra" time from their lifetime to others?

Media myths about teaching notwithstanding, most teachers would agree that they are really no different from any other individual trying to earn a living in a competitive society and a materialistic culture. Teachers have families, illnesses, car payments and older parents, and these obligations require time. In addition, as professionals, teachers have a hierarchy of material and psychological needs in the workplace that require time from their lifetime to address. The most important of these needs and the most time-consuming of all the activities in the lifetime of a classroom teacher is the time needed in the search for individual self-actualization or lifestyle satisfaction, or as we have come to know it, happiness. Teachers build their lifetimes with time investments, and time becomes the essence of the life process, as well as the change process at school. Finally, energy or effort, purpose or goals, and time expenditures combine in the lifetime of a classroom teacher to attain the goal of self-actualization, or happiness. The link between time and happiness is the main reason why some teachers are so possessive and protective of their time and why many recent efforts at school reform and change have failed.

The following are some of the relationships between time and the lifetimes of teachers that were alluded to in the previous two chapters. These relationships will be discussed in greater detail in this and subsequent chapters.

---

Teachers age on a linear clock, while the students they teach stay at approximately the same age over the teacher's career in the classroom.

---

- Teachers age on a linear clock, while the students they teach stay at approximately the same age over the teacher's career in the classroom (e.g., third-grade teacher, Algebra I teacher). For classroom teachers, this creates a major distortion in the sense of time passage because students seem static or frozen in time while they are aging in time. This is possibly why so many teachers feel younger than they actually are—they are always teaching students who never seem to age. Some consider this type of "time warp" in the classroom to be a major nonpecuniary benefit for the teaching profession and an extraordinary benefit that promotes both teacher satisfaction and lifestyle quality.

- Teachers have traditionally had a sense of time control over their job functions outside of the classroom, and in most cases they have control over how to allocate their time in the classroom setting itself. For many classroom teachers, time and time control are very positive aspects of the teaching profession. Personal control over time, therefore, is a major nonpecuniary benefit of classroom teaching.

- The cyclical time frame of the school organization and the linear time frame of the classroom teacher create major incentives for teachers who teach the same subject matter each year to front-load their school-teaching-related time investments in their early career. Then, if they choose, they can stick with their familiar classroom strategies and curriculum for the rest of their career in the classroom.

- Teachers have frequent breaks in their job functions (vacations, holidays, sick days, personal leave days) over the course of the academic year, and these time breaks often give them a unique position in the workforce. Time breaks, especially over the summer, permit teachers to pursue non-school-related time-consuming activities that might give them more lifestyle satisfaction, such as moonlighting or personal development and social activities.

- Because of personal time control and frequent time breaks, teachers, unlike other professionals in the workforce, can make choices regarding their investments of time for attaining lifestyle satisfaction. These time investments outside of the classroom setting can be used to further define their teaching persona and to find the personal self. Teachers can also be polychronometric with regard to time use, that is, have multiple compensations (material, social, personal) or uses for the same one hour of time.

• Some teachers feel that they are overworked and underpaid by the school organization. With time choices available outside of the school organization, many of these classroom teachers have the free time and the will to exercise these options to increase their lifestyle satisfaction.

• The quality of a teacher's life is reflected in his or her behavior in the classroom. Lifestyle quality that is based on the personal control of time and time investments indirectly affects student learning in the classroom via the behavior of the teacher.

This chapter specifically explores how the resource of time is used by classroom teachers both in and out of the school organization (see Table 3.1). Time, effort, and purpose (goals of lifestyle satisfaction) are an integral part of a teacher's decision-making framework and essentially govern his or her decision to participate in the extra time-consuming activities of the school organization. Many of these extra activities are associated with the school reform and change process; therefore, these activities also have to be accountable to the time, effort, and purpose criteria. Because there are competing time-consuming activities in the lifetime of a teacher, time becomes part of a decision-making rubric for engaging in school-related activities. Of course, when there are no alternatives for time engagement due either to economic conditions or physical-psychological conditions of the teacher, a default type of decision is made with regard to time investments.

Time investments needed by classroom teachers (a) to earn a living, (b) to maintain relationships, (c) to ensure personal development, and (d) for recovery or entertainment were defined and described in the previous chapter as being the four major parts of a time investment portfolio. *How and why certain time investments are emphasized in the lifetime of a teacher relate to the psychological, social, and physical needs of the teacher.*

Research conducted by Abraham Maslow (1943, 1970) described the hierarchy of personal needs that motivate human beings (see Figure 3.1). The time required to attend to each of these human needs

**TABLE 3.1** A Teacher's World of Time

| | |
|---|---|
| Linear time frame of aging | Finite amount of time—definite beginning, definite end, and definite interval |
| Energy or effort input | Convenience, fluency, technical skills, training, intelligence, energy expended— highly contextual, individual centered, and age related |
| Purpose or lifestyle satisfaction as a goal | Pursuit of happiness, self-actualization, individuation |
| Perceived benefits | Criteria for participation: material benefits, social relationship benefits, and personal development benefits |

in Maslow's hierarchy can be enormous. These needs force teachers to trade off various in-school and out-of-school time investments to ensure attaining the ultimate life goal of self-actualization. For example, certain time investments are needed to ensure physiological survival. At the next level, time investments are needed for personal safety in society. At the third level, time investments are needed for social approval and for developing a sense of belonging. At higher levels, time investments are needed and associated with the enhancement of self-esteem and ego status. The pinnacle of these human needs is what Maslow refers to as the self-actualization needs of an individual. As the pyramid structure suggests, the goal of self-actualization is primarily the result of prudent time investments made to the lower-level needs in the hierarchy.

Note how each of the levels of Maslow's hierarchy can be adapted to the classroom teacher. From job security to professional pride, and through the various levels of Maslow's hierarchy dealing with safety, belongingness, and ego status, classroom teachers have to invest their time to attain their ultimate goal in life: self-actualization.

Time-related fulfillment or self-actualization in adulthood has been examined as a series of passages over a lifetime (O'Connor & Woolfe, 1987; Shmotkin, 1991) and in case study formats (Colarusso, 1994). From this case study research, the important stages of adult development over a lifetime and their characteristic behaviors both

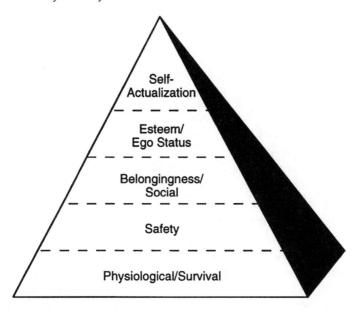

**Figure 3.1.** Hierarchy of Human Needs as Hypothesized by Maslow in His Typology
SOURCE: Maslow (1943, 1970).

inside and outside of work organizations have been generally defined as

1. Early adulthood (ages 17-45) or the age of maximum energy and physical capacity
2. Middle adulthood (ages 45-60) or the stage of beginning diminished capacity and midlife transition
3. Late adulthood (ages 60-70) or the stage of recognition of mortality, a continued decline in physical energy, and a shift from external focus to internal and personal needs focus
4. Very late adulthood (over 70) or the stage of rapid decline in energy, memory replacing vision, and personal focus replacing external focus of energy and thought

Although all of the above stages are important in the lifetime of a classroom teacher, the early and middle adult stages are most important with regard to school reform and change.

Classroom teachers tend to follow the following common time investment patterns of professional development over their lifespan and career in the classroom.

*Teachers aged 25-30.* This is the age where a teacher is investing time to try out different types of personas as a classroom teacher. This time period of a teacher's life is usually characterized by great amounts of energy and major time involvement and investment in school-related activities. At this age, time is also invested in experimenting with different lifestyle adventures while physical abilities are at a peak. Psychologically, and for most classroom teachers, there is an overall optimistic "glass is half full" attitude toward life. The main satisfaction for teachers at this stage of life comes from "living" characterized by high physical strength and low perceived time effort for a time-consuming activity. This implies that even if job satisfaction with teaching is low, a sufficiently high satisfaction to time effort (*S/TE*) ratio is maintained to ensure participation in school-related activities.

*Commentary.* Teachers in this age range are typically recent graduates from colleges or universities. The first ventures into the world of work as independent and single adults occur at this stage: new car, a new apartment, new sports and interests, new friends, and experimenting with different lifestyles that require time and money. The two great time investments in this period of development are typically work and social relationships.

*Teachers aged 30-40.* In this age range, a general maturity and refinement in the development of the classroom teacher persona are reached. Appropriate time investments in a teaching career lay important foundations for a serious commitment to the profession of a classroom teacher. This age usually provides the maximum *S/TE* ratios associated with the school organization and classroom teaching.

*Commentary.* Teachers in this age range are generally settling down in life, getting married and finding life partners to share their time. In this time period, they seek stable relationships in life both at work and in personal relationships.

*Teachers aged 40-50.* This is the beginning of a transition period for teachers between time needed for the development of the persona as a professional classroom teacher and time needed for the evolution of the self. At this stage of life, teachers need to get meaning from work to increase their satisfaction. Because there is typically an increase in time effort due to competing time-consuming activities in life and possibly declining physical capabilities, efforts to increase job satisfaction are important. In this age range we find the beginnings of the decline in *S/TE* ratios associated with school-related time-consuming activities, especially school reform and change efforts.

*Commentary.* At this age range, teachers may question past time investments in the teaching profession. A midlife crisis for these individuals also can be a crisis in time availability and lamentation over other previous time investments. The crisis in time often results in shifts in time investments from the world of work to personal interests and hobbies, or to family or health problems at home.

*Teachers aged 50-60.* Teachers at this age range want to do everything possible in life while still physically able to perform certain activities. There is an important time transition in these individuals from activities that merely fill time to time-consuming activities that are fulfilling. In some cases, a general pessimistic "glass is half empty" attitude begins to emerge in the personality. Many classroom teachers at this age in life begin to find that other non-school-related time-consuming activities provide higher *S/TE* ratios.

*Commentary.* At this stage of a teacher's life, the beginning of preparations for life outside of the world of work begins to emerge. There is also a continuation of shifts in time investments from work, or "selling time" activities, to interests and hobbies, or "spending time" activities. Finally, there is a continued decline in physical energy and a desire for comfort with low perceived time effort ratios in social and work relationships. Higher and higher levels of satisfaction must now be provided by the school organization to ensure participation of these teachers.

*Teachers aged 60 to retirement.* Finding "psychological 'passion' compensation" rather than "material compensation" in various time-consuming activities, usually outside of the world of work, characterizes classroom teachers at this age range. There is an important need for these teachers to reconcile problems with the past, find some exciting time-consuming activity to lose sleep over, or engage themselves in the future. Looking forward to life outside of the formal work in a school organization is typical of these teachers.

*Commentary.* At this age range, we see the beginning of the retirement phase of life. There is a concerted effort to try to find something they feel passionate about to provide interest for the rest of their lives. We also see the withdrawal of these teachers from the school organization and minimal time effort given for time-consuming activities at work. The golden parachute and early retirement orientation become important concerns. Psychologically, teachers are preparing for a "safe landing" away from the world of work in the school organization.

Teachers and their lifetimes in school organizations have been examined in the works of Lortie (1975) and Greenberg (1984). Specific relationships between teachers and the school organization with resulting behaviors such as plateauing in the school organization have been addressed in works by Bolman and Deal (1984), Hassard (1991), Milstein (1990a, 1990b), and Bardwick (1986).

Taking time from the lifetimes of teachers to service school reform efforts has not gone unnoticed in educational research. As one researcher noted: "It is neither fair nor wise to ask teachers to deduct to the reform and change effort in the school organization all the time needed from their personal lives even with compensation" (Raywid, 1993, p. 34).

Another researcher added insights on teachers' time effort in a classroom and familiarity with present teaching practices.

Familiar teaching repertoires have provided teachers with an economy of effort. Changes in schools that require new content and new repertoires for teaching are likely to be met with passive resistance by experienced teachers who have defined themselves an array of routines they can employ. (Eisner, 1992, p. 612)

The linkage between time and lifestyle satisfaction or quality of a teacher's life has also been examined and shown to be an important part of the school organizational climate. "The quality of life is measured by the amount of time control and free discretionary time one has available in life" (Adam, 1990, p. 94).

The linkage between age of an individual and time perceptions has also been explored. "Because older persons have longer temporal horizons or memories, a year appears as a temporal shorter distance to someone 80-years-old than someone eight-years-old" (Lewis & Weigert, 1981, p. 450).

Finally, the important linkage between time investments and risk has been noted from an economic perspective. "Age is positively associated with high average time preferences for psychologically fulfilling activities and high average risk aversions" (Leigh, 1986, p. 30).

Of course, for teachers who do not have any options with regard to investing time for either relationships or for personal development, it is quite easy to want to invest or sell nearly all of their available time to the school organization. It is not uncommon, therefore, for teachers in rural areas to make the school organizational setting the central focus of their lives. In essence, the school organization provides time-related economic, social, and personal development compensations for the classroom teacher, rather than the world outside of school. There are also workaholic types of teachers or selling-time teachers who have no life outside of school. In essence, these teachers merge their persona with the school organizational persona and thus actively participate in school-related activities until the end of a career in the classroom. *The one-dimensional, workaholic classroom teachers in a school might be appreciated by some school administrators because they are always willing to provide their time. One should question, however, whether this is the type of teacher that one would want teaching students or guiding school reform and change efforts.* With so little time investment, depth, and breadth in their own personal life experience, especially with regard to relationships and personal development, these classroom teachers might be psychologically incomplete and not the best role models for children or the best colleagues for other teachers. In fact, these teachers may contribute only a very narrow perspective of what is needed to promote school reform and change. More important, these teachers generally may not be sensitive to the time needs of other teachers, thus leading to resentment.

> Most psychologically healthy teachers search for a
> balanced, quality life, that is, a life filled with time-
> consuming activities that are both outside and inside
> of the school organization.

But most classroom teachers are not workaholics, are not narrow in time investments, and do have many alternative time-
consuming activities in their lives. Most psychologically healthy
teachers search for a balanced, quality life, that is, a life filled with
time-consuming activities that are both outside and inside of the
school organization and that have a balance between outer (selling
time), other (giving time), and inner (spending time) directness.
These teachers sense that they have a fixed amount of time in their
lifetimes to get what they want—earning a living, building relationships, developing talents, filling time—and thus act on these time
investments, even if it means placing school reform participation on
the back burner.

Following some of the notions of Maslow, the priority list of time
allocations or investments for classroom teachers can be ranked and
described as follows:

1. *Physical survival time:* time to address those activities that
   must get done, that is, time for taking care of life's necessities
2. *Economic survival time:* time for those activities needed to earn
   a living, that is, time for living a comfortable lifestyle
3. *Social survival time:* time to address those activities that are
   needed for social interaction and personal relationships, that
   is, time for friends and families
4. *Psychological survival and fulfillment time:* time to address the
   needs of the self, that is, time for personal development, recreation, and hobbies
5. *Consumptive time:* time to relax, recover, and be entertained,
   that is, nondirected time

Because of limited time availability, classroom teachers typically prioritize their time investments to maximize their overall lifestyle satisfaction. Methods used by teachers for prioritizing time generally

include developing classifications or a triage system of time investments similar to the following:

*Urgent—must do.* Here, the activity draws time from other activities in life. For example, work has to be completed on a report to the school board, so time is first taken from killing-time or filling-time activities (entertainment); second, time is taken from spending-time activities (hobbies and personal development); third, time is finally taken from giving-time activities (relationships and friends).

*Important—should do.* Here, the activity, although not directly taking time from other activities, becomes the dominant time-consuming activity within the selling-, giving-, spending-, and filling-time investment. For example, all the time allocated to giving-time investments is allocated to the family, and none of the time is allocated to developing or maintaining other relationships in life such as collegial relationships at school.

*Normal—can do.* Here, the activity reaches a steady state with other time-consuming activities in life, so the teacher can decide what time investments can be made in the selling, giving, spending, and filling time categories.

It is important to stress that it is possible for classroom teachers to develop strategies of being polychronometric with regard to their time investments in the school organization. For classroom teachers, the same 1 hour of time can serve two or three different objectives, and two or more different purposes or types of compensations and benefits in life: making money, enhancing social relationships, or personal development. ***The more polychronometric (multiuse) a teacher can make the time-consuming activity (reading a book while on an exercise cycle, grading papers at a faculty meeting), the higher the resulting satisfaction compensation for the activity.*** The $S/TE$ ratio thus increases, making the time investment activity more attractive for participation. This important principle of a multibenefit, split-screen approach to time, or polychronometric time, is an extremely important school leadership strategy that will be explored in later chapters (see Table 3.2).

**TABLE 3.2** A Split-Screen Approach to Time Investment

| | |
|---|---|
| Polychronometric time | Multiple uses in a lifetime for the same unit of time; a split-screen approach to life and view of time (reading while on an exercise cycle) |
| Monochronometric time | A single use for the same unit of time; a single-screen approach to life and view of life (giving a class lesson) |
| Examples of both types of time | Music teacher in classroom (outer-directed time) |
| | Music teacher in classroom writing a textbook on music and using the class for trying out ideas (outer- and inner-directed time) |
| | Music teacher in classroom writing a textbook on music and also developing relationships with students to assist in writing the book (outer-, inner-, and other-directed time) |

The downside to polychronometric time for classroom teachers, of course, is the diffusion of energy and the loss of pleasure that is associated with a split-screen approach to each of the activities. Rather than full attention, absorption, and pleasure in the single time-consuming activity, the intensity of a single activity is lessened. Of course, in many school organizational situations, lessening the intensity of a time-consuming activity is desirable (such as the boredom of an exercise cycle being relieved by reading, or the often wasted time at a faculty meeting being made more valuable by grading papers).

Finally, the question why some teachers allocate or invest their time at the minimum required levels of the school organization, whereas other teachers invest far more time than the minimum, is directly associated with the teachers' perceived $S/TE$ ratio. What complicates the problem for educational leadership is that these $S/TE$ ratios are not common to all teachers but are strongly influenced by the teacher's age, gender, subject matter specialty, and level of instruction, and the ethos of the school setting (urban, rural, suburban).

The extremely important linkage between time investments in life and happiness or lifestyle satisfaction is best described by the

**TABLE 3.3**  Linking Time Allocations and Happiness

---

If you want to be happy for a *moment,* have a drink.

If you want to be happy for an *hour,* take a nap.

If you want to be happy for a *day,* go fishing.

If you want to be happy for a *month,* get married.

If you want to be happy for a *year,* inherit some money.

If you want to be happy for a *lifetime,* enjoy your work.

---

Chinese proverb shown in Table 3.3. Note how this Chinese proverb places heavy emphasis on the investment of time at work (development of the persona) and lifetime happiness. Because the world of work—earning a living—consumes so much of an individual's time, it seems logical that time spent in the workplace is related to happiness. It is, therefore, important for educational leaders to examine time, work, and happiness linkages in classroom teachers. When teachers sign their teaching contract to teach in a classroom, they also assume that they are in control of their time. The only specified time required by the school organization is that of direct student contact or "contract" time. School reform and change activities that add many extra after-school, time-consuming activities, when overlaid on top of student contact time, can make overall school organizational time demands on a teacher much larger. The two ways that leadership can address these added time investment demands are by increasing $S$ or lowering $TE$.

  In summary, from the finite amount of time we are each given in a lifetime (approximately 700,000 hours in 80 years), teachers proceed to build their lifetimes with time. As the teacher progresses through life, the portfolio of the four basic directed types of time investments—selling, giving, spending, and filling time—changes until the teacher reaches what can best be described as a psychological comfort zone. Although the exact composition of the portfolio of time investments changes as we progress through life, the classifications of time allocations themselves tend to remain constant throughout a lifetime.

  To have a middle-class lifestyle, teachers must sell much of their time to school organizations to pay taxes, pay mortgages, meet car payments, feed families. Teachers also need to invest time to relax, work out, commute, have relationships, develop talents, engage in recreation, travel, read, have hobbies, raise children. It is important to examine the relationship of time to earning a living and teacher moonlighting both inside (e.g., extra tutoring) and outside (e.g., selling real estate) of the school organization.

## Time and Earning a Living as a Teacher

In a competitive market economy, one of the most important components of lifestyle satisfaction is the ability to earn a good living. Efforts to increase the salary options of classroom teachers have been reported in the literature (Gandera, 1992). When examining the market rate for a teacher's time, it is evident that the teaching profession has generally not kept up with the inflation rate. The use of time by teachers to achieve the lifestyle objective of earning a decent living is thus severely compromised, and the perceived benefit associated with extra, nonpaid school time investment is, therefore, quite low. The older, pushed-out, and marginalized teacher—at an age when individuals usually incur higher expenses such as medical costs and their children's college tuition—is particularly affected by inflation. In essence, time left in the career for these teachers will not allow them to recoup the financial loss caused by inflation. The impact of inflation on the erosion of savings and salaries via the decline in purchasing power can be psychologically devastating.

In the past and relative to salaries paid in other professions, the teaching profession offered what might be considered a decent middle-class standard of living. For past generations, earning a living at teaching was possible, and even one teacher's salary was generally enough to support a family and a middle-class lifestyle. Today, in many areas of the country, especially in large urban areas, two teacher salaries, even with no children, are often inadequate to support a middle-class lifestyle. Teachers, being intelligent, educated, and resourceful individuals, respond to this economic condition by wanting to sell more of their available time to the school organization (e.g., inside moonlighting, tutoring, running after-school programs, etc.) or sell their available time to other commercial organizations that have a higher market rate for their time (e.g., outside moonlighting).

As one classroom teacher noted,[1]

My biggest gripe with education today is that after teaching for 29 years, I was earning less than my nephew was earning 1 year out of law school. My biggest complaint is that we are here supposedly to educate and formulate how children are going to be. And we truthfully are the biggest day care providers, but if we were paid an hourly wage per child of baby-sitting we probably would earn more money than we do as teachers.

---

Even though teacher salaries are at their highest levels in history, the purchasing power associated with these salaries is much lower.

---

To better understand the need for classroom teachers to moonlight, one should appreciate that it is not the teachers' salary level itself that is important to consider but what the salary can purchase in an open-market economy. Even though teacher salaries are at their highest levels in history, the purchasing power associated with these salaries is much lower. The goods and services that present teacher salaries can purchase in today's market seem inadequate for many teachers to meet the needs of their middle-class lifestyle; hence, this lowering of purchasing power decreases the *S/TE* ratio and increases the propensity to moonlight. Correspondingly, declines in the purchasing power of teachers are also related to declines in the amounts of extra time given in the school organization by classroom teachers to support school reform and change efforts.

To appreciate the devastating impact inflation has on teacher salaries, consider the following simple illustration. Once again, note that it is the purchasing power, not the salary level for the teacher, that is the best economic measure of lifestyle satisfaction directed at earning a living.

Assume a starting salary for a teacher of $40,000 per year in 1990. In addition, assume a cost-of-living salary raise of 3% per year. The growth in salary for this teacher could be calculated by using the compound interest formula.

In 5 years, at an average cost-of-living raise of 3%, a classroom teacher would have a new salary of $40,000 $(1 + .03)^5$ or $40,000 (1.159) = $46,360$. But suppose the consumer price index or the inflation rate or the cost-of-living increase in the community was 6%. Then the value of each dollar would erode by the formula

$$V(t) = \frac{1}{(1+6\%)^t}$$

$$V(t) = \frac{1}{(1+.06)^5}$$

$$V(t) = \frac{1}{1.338}$$

$$V(t) = .747$$

Thus, although the classroom teacher might be earning substantially more salary ($46,360 vs. $40,000) in the school organization, each dollar of salary has been devalued (1.00 vs. 0.75) and the purchasing power lowered. The actual purchasing power for the classroom teacher or the true measure of earning a living, for the time provided and for purposes of lifestyle satisfaction, would then be $46,360 (.75) = $34,770.

Thus, the real earning power of the classroom teacher has actually declined ($40,000 vs. $34,770, or $5,230). Stated differently, the cost to the teacher for being in the classroom is $5,230. Paying $5,230, or a 13% cut in salary, for the privilege of being a classroom teacher does not typically enhance lifestyle satisfaction. In addition, this hidden "tax" of inflation is not very conducive for ensuring teacher participation in the extra time-consuming, after-school activities associated with school reform and change. Given the sensitivity of the $S/TE$ ratio to participation, a 13% decline in $S$ has to at least be offset by 13% decline in $TE$.

Declines in purchasing power, of course, will predispose classroom teachers to supplement their income by moonlighting; at worst, teachers might moonlight outside of school. At best, teachers might moonlight in nonmaterial ways, by using extra time for recreation and hobbies and for friends and families. Regardless of the objective of moonlighting time (material, social, or personal compensation), the net result is the same: Teachers will make a minimal time commitment to the school organization, because the "returns"

**TABLE 3.4** Economic Worth of Teachers' Time

|            | Teacher Salary | Daily Rate | Hourly Rate | Rate per Minute |
|------------|----------------|------------|-------------|-----------------|
| Pretax     | $30,000        | $166.67    | $27.78      | $.46            |
| After tax  | 15,000         | 83.30      | 13.80       | .23             |
| Pretax     | 40,000         | 222.22     | 37.04       | .62             |
| After tax  | 20,000         | 111.11     | 18.50       | .31             |
| Pretax     | 50,000         | 277.78     | 46.20       | .77             |
| After tax  | 25,000         | 138.00     | 23.00       | .38             |

NOTE: Assume (a) a 180-day school year; (b) after total taxes (state, federal, local, and sales); (c) additional cost at an overall marginal tax rate of 50%; and (d) a 6-hour school day.

on their time investments (economic and psychological) are higher in these other, outside-of-school time-consuming activities.

The question, "Is the school reform activity worth my time?" from an economic perspective is illustrated in Table 3.4.

Thus, when answering the question of whether the reform activity is worth the time, one has to first examine the taxable economic worth to time, then the competing taxable economic worth or moonlighting time. The nontaxable psychological worth of other (relationship), inner (personal development), and nondirected (recovery or consumptive) types of time investments also has to be included in the analysis.

Teachers moonlighting outside of the school organization engage in a wide variety of jobs, from bartender to massage therapist to real estate agent. Some of these jobs might be demeaning; others serve as alternative careers and are very attractive. Available time to earn extra income can thus become a major pecuniary objective of a classroom teacher. There are even books written on the subject of how to moonlight, such as *How to Teach School and Make a Living at the Same Time* (Crowe, 1978). "Some teachers do not moonlight for the money but for personal fulfillment of participating in some sort of socially beneficial extracurricular activity. [In one study,] of all teachers holding second jobs, 88% worked because of economic necessity" (Bell & Roach, 1990, p. 10).

Moonlighting teachers have very little time for school reform efforts. In a study of Kansas teachers, more than half held paying positions outside of school (Alley, 1990).

Many teachers report an outside income of less than $5,000 in a year. The amount of time spent by those moonlighting teachers to supplement their incomes also varies greatly. Seventy-one percent of teachers worked a maximum of 20 additional hours per week. Twenty-five percent reported working 25 to 40 hours per week. Four percent reported working more than 40 hours a week in addition to their teaching position. (Bell & Roach, 1990, p. 9)

Some school systems are so poorly funded that teachers often have to use their own out-of-pocket resources, thus lowering satisfaction. According to a study of Texas schoolteachers, "A startling 96% said that lack of funds was forcing them to spend an average of $250 of their own money to support classroom activities" (Henderson, 1994, p. 6).

One classroom teacher who moonlights outside of the school organization rationalizes his behavior as follows:

I am a fourth-grade teacher at an elementary school in California. I moonlight on the side by involving myself in a catering business on the weekends. I am single and want to earn as much money as I can so that I can afford travel to Europe and a new car. I moonlight because I like the extra income, and it really does not affect my ability to teach, because I moonlight on the weekends.

## Time and the Personas of Classroom Teachers

Certain situations in life make some classroom teachers want to invest more of their time participating in school reform and change activities, whereas other teachers are not the least bit interested in participating. Guilt, professional obligation, pride, the teaching persona that is projected as part of the job, and colleague pressure all have an effect on the choice to participate or not. The time investment portfolio and the teacher's perceived *S/TE* ratio associated with the extra time-consuming activity, however, are most important to understanding participation. Specifically, the teacher's perceived consumptive and investment benefits, along with the actual amount of time available for the activity, can have a great influence on the predisposition of a teacher to participate.

The following are some of the investment or consumptive benefits for a teacher participating in a school organization's extra time-consuming activity.

First, a teacher might want to learn more about the activity to enhance his or her status or economic worth in the school organization. In other words, a time investment is made to sell time to the school organization at a higher rate in the future. Additionally, it is possible that thoughts of later moving from the classroom to school administration and wanting to be noticed as a leader by administrators can provide motivation to participate. Typically, younger teachers in the school organization would have the most to gain from this type of time investment benefit.

Second, a teacher might want to meet a friend or use the activity as an opportunity for social bonding with other teachers. Here, the notion of time takes on a polychronometric nature because one can use the same quantitative amount of time to generate dual benefits, that is, to get to know someone better and to learn about a school reform activity.

Third, a teacher might have always been personally interested, from a creative, professional, or intellectual standpoint, in the time-consuming activity, and for personal development reasons wants to learn more about its use in the school organization.

Fourth, a teacher might have had absolutely nothing better to do with his or her time in life and therefore used this time-consuming activity as a filler. Here, time is used as a consumptive benefit. A consumptive-benefit view of time investment in the reform activity, although somewhat rare in school organization, does occur.

The personas of classroom teachers are strongly related to the types of time investments made to competing time-consuming activities in life, that is, outer-directed teachers, other-directed teachers, and inner-directed teachers.

## The Outer-Directed Teacher:
## Organization and Career Centered

*Material Compensation Goal: "Time Is Money"*

The outer-directed teacher generally invests time in those activities that lead to material or career compensation and recognition by the school organization. Teachers desiring an advanced degree purely to move up in the salary schedule, teachers wishing to pursue careers in school administration, and teachers who want to be compensated for all extra time needed by the school organization are outer directed in their views toward time investments. These are the time investments that are needed to enhance teacher status, salary, and prestige and are generally associated with earning a living.

School reform and change activities, of course, can be made suitable to outer-directed teachers if there is a potential for a sufficient gain in position, career status, or material and financial rewards. Unfortunately, as teachers age, outside-of-school outer-directed time investments become more important.

Here is how one outer-directed teacher summarized his time investment in the school organization:

> I volunteer my time for everything I can. I get involved and make my superiors know of my presence. One must "play the game," so to speak, in order to project oneself into the role of an administrator. I have been involved as an athletic coach (baseball), club adviser (Letterman's Club), and participated and/or chaired numerous faculty committees. I am volunteering for numerous activities in order to set myself up for an opening in school administration. The concerns of the student body are not always at the top of my list for participating.

Reflections of a graduate student toward teachers perceived to be outer directed provide a compelling description of the "time is money" personas in the school organization:

> I have had the experience of taking several seminars relating to my particular field of interest and was always attending seminars in order to enhance my knowledge. The person conducting

the seminar was an expert, very experienced, with a solid reputation of success.

The most common skill that these types of outer-directed teachers seem to have is time management skills in the organization. The way these teachers spoke, distributed materials, managed the schedule of the seminar, all happened within a very structured time format. Furthermore, in most cases these teachers identified time management as a critical skill.

## The Other-Directed Teacher: Student and Social Centered

*Compensation and Social Relationship Goal:*
*"Time Not Given to Kids Is Time Wasted"*

The other-directed teacher generally invests time in time-consuming activities that are associated with the caring and social relationships that are part of the profession of teaching. These teachers usually freely give their time to the multitude of extra time-consuming activities at school, especially if these activities are aimed at improving the lives of children and establishing relationships with fellow teachers. Teachers who, on their own time, share their materially uncompensated time with students and fellow teachers develop the persona of an other-directed or "giving time" teacher.

Time-consuming activities for school reform and change, unless they are fully and demonstrably helpful to children, might be ignored by other-directed teachers. Although they are not opposed to school reform and change, other-directed teachers typically don't lead the school change process either.

Sometimes other-directed teachers have enormous time pressures from their other relationships in life (other than students and fellow teachers), and they have to adjust their time investments accordingly.

As one teacher noted,

I am married with a 21-month-old son and on an average school day, excluding time spent on school-related activities and sleeping, I have 3 or 4 hours at the most to spend with my family. On weekends I like to spend at least 1 day not doing anything having to do with school. I spend on average 4 hours at school every Sunday.

A graduate student, in describing an other-directed teacher, noted,

> In my case, I was fortunate to have been in contact with several teachers who volunteered their time for out-of-classroom activities. Both as a student and now as a parent, I feel very fortunate to have been exposed to these types of teachers. More than learning skills, volunteer teachers helped me to learn to get along with other types of people. They took time out of their schedules. Even though I did not realize it at the time, somehow I knew their presence meant something. They created a family type setting that made learning more comfortable and desirable.

Fortunately, the profession of teaching is dominated by individuals who are other directed, especially at the elementary school level. In fact, most teachers enter the profession for both time benefits and the human benefits associated with helping children, social bonding to others, and building relationships. Therefore, for these classroom teachers, time investments that make the student-teacher relationship better in a school organization are typically sought with regard to professional development. By giving time, the impact of other-directed teachers at the secondary school level can be enormous, because many students at the high school level crave this time and attention from their teachers. Another graduate student noted,

> Mrs. W was my math teacher for 2 years, for both geometry and precalculus. From the moment I met her, I could sense that she was a caring teacher and sincerely concerned about her students learning. In the classroom, she had perfectly prepared lessons, with great interaction between herself and the students. Students had no fear of asking questions when confused about the concepts being introduced, because everyone knew that Mrs. W would treat them with the utmost respect and continue explaining until the problem was clear to everyone. As a teacher, she made sure that each and every student understood the concept being taught before she moved on to the next topic, even if it meant changing her lesson plan.

## *The Inner-Directed Teacher: Self-Centered*

*Personal Development Goals: "This Time Is My Time"*

The inner-directed teacher typically invests time in time-consuming activities in the school organization that are required for personal development, sports, hobbies, recreation, and personal interests. The profession of teaching is used by these teachers as a vehicle for both personal growth and material compensation. For example, art teachers, language teachers, and those teachers using technology to support their own private, inner-world interests wish to spend more time on their own personal benefit while being paid (polychronometric or multiple use of time).

Inner-directed teachers are usually subject matter specialists and are most often found teaching at the secondary level. Classroom teaching by many inner-directed teachers becomes an extension of their private interests. The persona of the teacher is not a "teacher" as such, but a subject matter specialist who teaches.

Sometimes single and unmarried teachers become heavily involved in their personal development activities, but as they progress in the school organization they become forced to make choices with regard to their time investments.

One middle school teacher noted,

> I have no family to share my personal time with. I am involved in dirt bike racing and had, at one point, begun to consistently place in the top five in every race, beating some of the sponsor's team riders. This is the only true non-school-related activity that I enjoy, and even this I have quit doing for lack of practice time. My typical schedule is: arrive at school at 6:30 a.m., teach until 3:00 p.m., coach until 6:30 p.m., set up for lab (usually 2 hours), type out, hand out, and grade papers, which, if you assume you only spend 1 minute per paper (which is usually inadequate) with 150 students, you can count on it taking at the very minimum, 2 $\frac{1}{2}$ hours. I am also enrolled in 16-20 semester units per year, a venture which I began while earning my credential in California.

Inner-directed or spending-time teachers are interested in school reforms that might lead to an intellectual or personal development growth. Helping students and organizational efficiency might therefore take second place to the effect that the reform has on their own particular professional development—usually in a specific subject matter area.

A teacher training student noted,

> Overall, Dr. M was a good lecturer in that he discussed a large amount of material. Unfortunately, many students would say that his lectures are not very exciting. He simply stood in front of the class and presented the information to the students in a monotonous voice for 50 minutes. At the beginning of each class, he would give one "pop quiz" question that counted as extra points on the exams. Through this he ensured student attendance, but was not really testing the students' knowledge. He was into his own thing.

Inner-directed teachers can also have an important impact on those students who share the same subject matter interest of the teacher.

As one high school teacher noted,

> Because of my subject matter (industrial arts), which I love, I spend a considerable amount of personal time on keeping up with the field. I teach a photography class at this school because it is also my hobby. As a result of my passion for the subject, 10 years ago I built a darkroom out of one of the bathrooms in my house.

Note that the personal time and resources that this teacher spent on this project were considerable, but the teacher also received a high amount of satisfaction for the amount of time effort invested.

In situations that are most successful, inner-directed teachers find mechanisms to share and be paid for this personal development experience.

Finally, there is a powerful and natural urge on the part of classroom teachers to want to spend more of their time on the development of the self in an inner-directed, private manner. This is especially true as teachers age and as their perceived work and family responsibilities lessen. Here is one teacher who feels a lessening of the burdens of family:

When my youngest child finally got her driver's license, I couldn't believe how much more time I had for myself. So I was able to enroll in school, and now I am working for my master's degree. I still spend a great deal of time with my family, but now I want to spend it on myself.

Another teacher at the same school site spends his released time in pursuit of spiritual reflection:

Being involved in church has always been a major role for my life. I don't let a day go by without spending time on my religious beliefs. This is not time that I am willing to give up, because it gives me inner peace. I don't think I could be an effective teacher if I did not have my own daily ritual of going to church.

Note that private time, whether it is spent on hobbies, recreation, talents, or spiritual pursuits, is needed to refresh the spirit of the teacher.

## Teachers at Midlife: Changes in the Sense of Time Passage Over a Teaching Career

As noted previously, the mechanism that produces the inner-, outer-, and other-directed persona of a classroom teacher and that one uses to find the self in later life is the investment of time. How these time investment choices are made becomes an interesting question for school leaders because it entails teachers' perceptions of time effort along with their perception of benefits. The time effort ($TE$) or "fluency" and the satisfaction ($S$) or compensation derived (material, social, personal), therefore, are strongly associated with time investment. The $S/TE$ ratio not only draws the teacher to the time-consuming activity (attractiveness), but it also results in the stimulating of information-seeking behaviors on the part of the teacher to support the activity throughout the career, that is, it keeps the teacher bonded to the activity.

Older classroom teachers have invested much time in their teaching and are typically fluent at their teaching tasks. These teachers are naturally reluctant to change something that is already working for them in the classroom or that is giving them high satisfaction

**TABLE 3.5** Factors Affecting Older Teachers and Their Satisfaction
in the School Organization (perceived benefits)

| | |
|---|---|
| Subject matter changes | More time needed to keep up with subject matter, especially in the areas of science and technology (more time effort [TE] needed, but possibly more satisfaction [S]) |
| Students changing | Students get more difficult to teach in the classroom each year |
| | Higher marginal cost due to family and social dysfunction in the community (more TE, less satisfaction) |
| School organization changes | Organizations that are uncaring and don't reward good teachers |
| | Politics of the workplace |
| | Teachers "cruise" to the minimum expected performance standards (less TE, low satisfaction) |

to the time effort needed. In many situations, satisfaction (loosely termed to mean "what is in it" for teachers in terms of benefits) to time effort (loosely termed to imply cost to teachers in terms of time and effort) with any proposed school change or reform might result in a $S/TE$ ratio that is lower. *Because many older teachers do not plan to be in the teaching profession much longer, there is a natural tendency for these teachers to resist any school reform effort that changes the way they presently do things in the classroom.* The reluctance to change is especially apparent if they feel that they won't be in the classroom long enough to reap any of the expected benefits. If the classroom teacher has reached a career plateau in the school organization, then most attempts at school reform will be opposed or ignored unless they can dramatically increase their present $S/TE$ ratio in the classroom (see Table 3.5).

As noted earlier, the subjective weighted hour or the ratio of time spent to time remaining as a classroom teacher matures in the school organization is another important time concept for educational leaders to consider. The subjective weighted hour directly relates to the $S/TE$ ratio because the perception, feel, or sense of time passage increases, thus lowering the $S/TE$ ratio. Because the $TE$ portion of the ratio tends to automatically increase with classroom teacher age, engaging older teachers in school reform efforts is particularly challenging for educational leaders.

The following are two important reasons why *TE* is perceived by classroom teachers to increase with age:

1. Physiological changes (sight or hearing impairments, declining energy, declining health) make performing teaching tasks more time-consuming and difficult.
2. The "how" of the teaching profession itself changes, requiring additional time investment to accommodate to different types of curriculums, students, and school organizations.

Note how the ratio of time lived to time left in life in a teaching career changes dramatically as the teacher ages. As noted earlier, and for purposes of illustration, to engage an average teacher who is 50 years old in a 1-hour after-school activity is quite a bit more challenging than engaging an average 20-year-old teacher. The 50-year-old teacher senses that this 1 hour of time is subjectively weighted as 5 hours of time (1.66/.35). Stated differently, the teacher asks if a 1-hour after-school organization activity is really worth a perceived 5-hour investment of time. The weight itself is derived from the ratio of time lived to time remaining over an average 80-year life span (see Table 3.6).

In short, educational leaders cannot expect participation in extra time-consuming school reform activities of teachers from different age groups to be equal. An understanding of the subjective or weighted time to a teacher should become a basic premise of school leadership in an era of time scarcity. For example, effective leadership in an era of time scarcity would ask the question, "Is the 1-hour meeting worth 1.66 hours for the 50-year-old teacher?" (Note that the same 1-hour meeting has the value of .35 hours or 22 minutes for a 21-year-old teacher.)

Older teachers, being secure in their teaching, have typically developed a bag of teaching tricks they use in an effort to create teaching fluency in the classroom and thus lower their *TE*. Because some older teachers do not see themselves as moving up in the salary structure of the school organization, and because they have job security via tenure, these teachers have essentially reached a career plateau. At this stage of a teaching career, they are far more likely to invest their time in personal and non-school-related time-consuming

**TABLE 3.6** Weighted Value of Time as a Function of Age

| Time-Consuming Activity | 20-Year-Old (weighted) (.35) | 50-Year-Old (weighted) (1.66) |
|---|---|---|
| One-hour meeting | 22 minutes | 1.66 hours |
| Half-day, 4-hour workshop | 1.2 hours | 6.6 hours |
| One-day seminar | 2.8 hours | 13.3 hours |
| One-week institute | 14 hours | 66.4 hours |
| One-year illness | 4 months | 1.66 years |

activities (earning extra money, hobbies and personal interests, friends and family) because these activities yield higher satisfaction.

Midlife for a classroom teacher is typically a source of great pain. At midlife comes the realization that there is not enough time left in life to gratify all of the personal wishes (professional and nonprofessional). Naturally, midlife for an average teacher makes time in the present urgent and valuable. At midlife, teachers also tend to want to trade their selling-time investments to the school organization for more spending-time personal development investments (from outer to inner directness) or giving-time investments (from outer to other directness). In fact, if these teachers could buy back some of the time they "sold" to the school organization in their early careers, they probably would.

In school settings with large numbers of preretirement teachers in the age range of 50 to 65, school reform and change efforts are extremely difficult to implement because of the higher, or weighted, value placed on present time. Educational leaders have traditionally dealt with this problem by marginalizing or otherwise pushing out these classroom teachers from the reform and change effort. Unfortunately, this practice removes any sense of memory of effective past educational practices from the school reform debate. The school reform effort thus becomes incomplete and aligned to only those teachers who participate.

The pushed-out teacher or the marginalized teacher who is not participating is not behaving unprofessionally, but is reflecting the fact that the S/TE ratio is too low to engage in the extra time-consuming activity. Participation is simply not worth their time effort.

These teachers might actually wish to participate in the professional development activity, but the current level of satisfaction is too low or the time commitment and effort demanded by the school organization is too high. School organizations have to do something about both satisfaction and time effort for these veteran teachers to ensure their participation in school reform and change efforts.

Younger teachers in the school organizations, who provide important vision for the future, participate in school reform because they are the future of the school organization. The hope of these teachers is that their participation time in the present will pay off in the future with regard to delivery of instruction, that is, the reform will result in higher satisfaction or compensation and lower time effort so that the $S/TE$ ratio would be higher than in the present. In addition, because they are younger, the subjective sense of time itself is lower, hence automatically lowering the perception of time effort needed in the school organization. Finally, for younger teachers, there are definite possibilities for advancement or career development benefits in the school organization because of their participation in school reform and change activities.

Leaders should develop strategies that involve both older and younger teachers so that a combination of memory and vision is provided to the school reform debate.

Naturally, what is required by educational leaders in an era of time scarcity is to develop strategies that involve both older and younger teachers so that a combination of memory and vision is provided to the school reform debate.

When teachers are marginalized by the school organization because of their lack of time to engage in reform efforts, professional resentment and anger usually result. Because these teachers have already made a substantial commitment of time to the profession early in their career, they feel that their past time investment has been devalued. Professional isolation of these teachers can then create a hostile and suspicious environment for reform and change to occur in the school organization. Isolation of teachers at school also creates incentives for these teachers to invest their time in activities outside of the school organization (moonlighting). In addition, these pushed-out teachers can sabotage, vehemently oppose, or bad-mouth any reform effort that affects their present teaching practice.

## Summary

It has long been suggested that many classroom teachers entered the teaching profession precisely because they valued the opportunity to exercise personal control over their time. For some of these teachers, control over one's time in life was an important benefit (a nonpecuniary benefit) that might be of equal value to the benefit of salary (a pecuniary benefit).

The nature of the teaching profession is such that time required for teaching can be planned and that a life outside of the classroom can be adjusted accordingly. The locus of control, therefore, over one's time becomes a key element in the implicit contract between classroom teachers and the school organization. In fact, time control by teachers might eventually become a major point of conflict in collective bargaining negotiations between unions and school organizations in the future.

Some of the most vociferous opponents to school change and restructuring efforts are teachers themselves. These dissenters simply do not want to give or even sell their time to support the change and reform process. The subjective weighted hour, a concept developed in this chapter, offers a partial explanation to the attitude toward participation in extra time investments in the school organization, especially for veteran teachers. An understanding of the nature of time perceptions and investments of classroom teachers thus has direct relevance for not only enhancing the effectiveness of educational leaders but also for making the school organization a more psychologically accommodating and nurturing place to work.

In an era of time scarcity, professional development time in many situations has to accommodate to the other lifestyle goals and objectives of the classroom teacher. A teacher working out to stay healthy and stay in shape for the rigorous physical demands of the teaching profession, a teacher with a long commute because of the lack of availability of affordable housing near the school site, or a teacher with family obligations and responsibilities is not very likely to want to add extra hours to the workday by participating in school reform and change activities. It's concern about *time*, and not about the lack of classroom teacher professionalism, that accounts for many of the observed teacher behaviors of commitment, burnout, and dropout in school organizations. It is the lack of time and, more important, the lack of satisfaction derived to the time effort expended that should be the principal concern of school leaders. The *S/TE* ratio, therefore, becomes an important measure for understanding the participation rate of teachers in the multitude of extra time-consuming activities that are associated with reform and change efforts in a school organization.

## Perspectives, Points of View, Discussion

- Do you feel that there is a linkage between the worth of one's time as a classroom teacher (pay scale) and the feeling of personal worth in the school organization?
- Do you feel that the value of one's time to others in the school organization can be considered an independent measure of worth to the organization and others? If yes, what are the implications of time worth of teachers to school reform activities?
- Do you think the type of watch a classroom teacher uses (digital, face, no watch) reflects his or her perspective with regard to time and the teacher's past, present, and future time orientations?
- With regard to time needed for school change and reform, are there any differences between school moonlighting (after-school paid work) and outside-of-school moonlighting (after-school paid work)?
- In your experience, what are some of the ways that teachers invest their out-of-school time? Does this pattern seem to change with the age of the teacher?
- Do you consider control over one's time to be a major psychological principle in life and one of the major nonpecuniary benefits of teaching?

# NOTE

1. This quote and other quotes in this chapter, unless otherwise noted, are from extensive interviews conducted with hundreds of teachers and graduate students. Teachers from rural, suburban, and urban school settings participated in a time study to get a clearer picture of how time affects the lifetime of a teacher and, more specifically, how efforts on school reform and change affect teacher time.

# 4

# Structuring Teacher Time in School Organizations

*Each generation imagines itself to be more intelligent than the one that went before it and wiser than the one that comes after it.*

GEORGE ORWELL

---

- Time Needs of School Organizations
- Structuring Teacher Time in School Organizations
- Summary
- Perspectives, Points of View, Discussion

---

## Time Needs of School Organizations

---

The school organization is the major claimant of time in the lifetime of a teacher. An important measure of self-worth for a teacher, therefore, is in direct relation to the economic, social, and personal development worth of their time investment in the school organization.

---

Many work organizations in the private sector, in an effort to gain more profit, increase market share, or enhance their legitimacy as an institution, will attempt to "purchase" all of the time available from their employees. Increasing salaries, threatening layoff, and elevating professional status in the company are some of the methods organizations use to coerce additional individual time investments. With many downsized companies, the additional workload on remaining employees has increased enormously. In addition, these organizations have begun to use contract workers instead of regular, full-time employees, leading to hidden-cost problems of sabotage and security. For the privilege of having a job and, sometimes, but not always, an increase in salary, it is not uncommon for a full-time, professional employee in the private sector to work 15 to 18 hours per day.

The school organization interested in reform and change has to also request additional time from its teachers. Due to financial conditions in the school organization, however, many schools cannot purchase this extra needed time. The fact that job tenure ensures a position for the teacher, regardless of the time needed by the organization, compounds the problem for educational leaders. Even if the school organization could purchase the extra needed time for reform and change, there are many situations where some classroom teachers would simply be unwilling to provide the time because they would rather engage in other non-school-related activities. Unlike many other professionals, teachers simply have a choice. *Getting teachers to voluntarily provide the extra time needed to plan and design school reform during the school day and school year is particularly problematic for school leaders. Even classroom teachers who are idealistically and professionally motivated would find it difficult to provide all the needed time because of time demands from their families and outside interests.*

School organizations have attempted to formally structure teachers' time during the day, or contract time, by the use of lesson plans, class schedules, and school calendars. But school reform and change efforts require that classroom teachers give added or outside-of-formal-contract time. Educational leaders are thus faced with the immense challenge of how to get teachers to give this extra needed time.

As we approach the 21st century, it is not an overstatement to suggest that a major claimant to a classroom teacher's time is not the student but the school organization. The claim on teachers' time has increased steadily over the past several decades due to important changes in societal expectations and demands for reform and change. Changes in the locus of time control from the individual classroom teacher to the school organization might become one of the most important legacies of the school reform movement. Changes in time control might also loom as a major collective bargaining issue between teacher unions and school organizations in the future. Lesson plans, school schedules, school calendars, after-school conferences, school site management, and yearly events are typical of the efforts by school organizations to structure and claim the time of teachers.

The following are some of the relationships among time, teachers, and the school organization that will be addressed in this chapter.

• School organizations attempt to empower teachers by giving them a certain amount of ownership over time in their classrooms (contract time), certain courses in the curricula, and specific subject matter areas. Actual allocation of time in the formal classroom setting, therefore, is still mainly controlled by teachers.

• School organizations are characterized by short-term school board members and central administration staffs (transient over time), and long-term classroom teachers (permanent over time). This creates a time situation in the school organization where teachers can wait out any administrative demands for extra time needed for school reforms and change.

• Schools use class schedules, school calendars, lesson plans, and regular monthly events in an attempt to control the time of teachers. This sets up an implicit condition whereby if time is not fully specified for the classroom teacher by the school organization, all time outside of formal contract time is assumed to be free or discretionary.

• Teachers' salaries are based on a narrow view of time, such as years of classroom teaching experience, and a narrow view of time investments, such as time invested in college units or highest college degree. This results in a situation for classroom teachers where surviving the school organization and taking college courses is better compensated than being productive or effective in the classroom. Ideas for modifications of the fixed-step salary schedule to create better incentives for teachers to provide the needed time will be presented in Chapter 6.

- Educational leaders' requests for technological innovations, as well as other school reforms, are usually added slowly and over long time periods in a piecemeal fashion. This results in a situation of having a sub-critical mass needed for "time appropriate" change in the school organization; that is, a head of steam for reform and change never develops in the school organization.

- Time management skills or getting more time into the day of a teacher—although valued by educational leaders—has a limited effect on the classroom behavior of teachers. Lifetime management or getting more life into the time of teachers so that they can better influence student learning might result in a greater impact on participation rates for teachers in school reform.

- School organizations are generally placed in an adversarial position with regard to classroom teachers and time control. Classroom teachers generally feel that educational leaders should pay teachers for all the time needed for school reform, that is, the time needed for reform and change is not in the formal teaching contract and is, therefore, discretionary.

- School organizations generally use time as a resource input to the process of schooling. School reforms are then evaluated for importance to the mission or goals of the school. Teachers use time as an output (happiness, lifestyle satisfaction) to the process of schooling to be evaluated for its worth in promoting lifestyle satisfaction. There is an inherent conflict between teacher time and school organization time.

- When dealing with school calendar reform, there is sometimes minor opposition by teachers to year-round schools because of their two 2-month vacation time periods. There is almost universal opposition to extending school days and school years because of the implications for time and its resulting encroachment on other time-consuming activities in a teacher's life.

Even though teachers have a great deal of personal time control in the classroom, the school organization still has the power to control, via course assignment and school placement, the satisfaction received by the teacher and contract time effort required in the school setting. This results in a situation of codependence where teachers and school organizations can either both lose or both gain with regard to time and time investment. The challenge for educational leaders in an era of time scarcity, therefore, is to consider and appreciate teacher time from a win-win time investment perspective. This is a difficult challenge to address in a typical school setting because the profession of teaching is extremely sensitive to intergenerational time attitudes, time perceptions, and time investments. *Leading both younger and older classroom teachers to school reform, at the same school site, could be quite difficult, because time values, time investments, and time perceptions of younger teachers might be quite different from those of older teachers.* One reason for this discrepancy is based on the concept of the subjective weight given to time itself (the ratio of time lived to time remaining is different between younger and older teachers). The second reason might be that the older teacher lived and was trained in a different generation and so had values toward time, time control, and time investments in the school organization that might be totally different from today's generation of teachers. In short, the effective educational leader not only understands the present time period of the school organization but also understands and appreciates the time periods of all teachers at the school site—older teachers, middle-aged teachers, and younger teachers.

The age of the teachers can have a major influence on their values toward time and time investments. The World War II traditionalists (age 55 and older), the in-betweeners (age 45-54), the challengers (age 35-44), and the synthesizers and pragmatists (age 25-34) share a relatively common perspective toward life and the world of work within their generation, but are distinctly different from those outside of their generation (Massey, 1979). How time interacts with these intergenerational clusters of teachers is given some attention in this book, but it has been explored in depth in the general context of time in work organizations (Bluedorn & Denhardt, 1988; Cushman, 1990; Hassard, 1991; Massey, 1979; McGrath & Rotchford, 1983). Specific examination of time in school organizations has been presented in the works of Ben-Peretz and Bromme (1990), Donahoe (1993), and Fortman (1984).

As noted in the educational research literature, control of class-room teacher time by school organizations is strongly related to their perceived power and influence over teachers.

The use and control of time by school organizations in interaction with the classroom teacher is also important to examine. The manner in which time is manipulated and the rationales for the introduction of changes are evidence of how power and influence is exercised in educational organizations. (Ben-Peretz & Bromme, 1990, p. 261)

The important link between teacher time expectations for a career as a classroom teacher and the purpose of time toward increasing lifestyle satisfaction is also interesting to investigate—especially regarding teachers who have reached their ceiling of advancement or have been plateaued by the school organization.

The career path has immense psychological significance for the classroom teacher because it ties past time investments with present time investments. Both past and present components are associated with teachers' behaviors and a personal vision of their future in the classroom. "Careers give an individual an acute sense of social time and we evaluate ourselves in terms of a career path that includes states of the past, present and future" (Hassard, 1991, p. 112).

Finally, the important linkage between individual time and organizational time has recently been given greater importance in educational research that deals with the management of the change process. "Time is central to evolutionary models of change. It is used as a resource to account for early innovation and in social relationships. It is posited as the connecting link between observed differences in social organizations" (Heirich, 1964, p. 393).

---

The era of the previous generation of teachers who had jobs defined by contract as being from 8 a.m. to 3 p.m. for 180 days is rapidly ending.

---

The next generation of classroom teachers, when looking back over their present teaching practices, will be in a better position to appreciate (and evaluate) how profoundly the school organization has changed attitudes toward teacher time control over the past several decades. What schools are presently experiencing with regard to teachers not wanting to participate in extra time-consuming school reform and change activities is merely a transition period in U.S. public education. The era of the previous generation of teachers who had jobs defined by contract as being from 8 a.m. to 3 p.m. for 180 days is rapidly ending. More time is now being required from teachers in an open contract format, not only for teaching students in the classroom but also for the large amounts of paperwork and extra time that surrounds management at a school site. Added to the time burden of classroom teachers are societal recommendations for longer school days and longer school years. Thus, for classroom teachers, there is a major difference between psychological contracts (Rousseau, 1989), implied contracts, formal contracts, and so forth. These perceptions of the teaching contract can lead to wide variations in the degrees to which teachers are willing to provide time needed to service the demands of school reform.

In addition to clock time, year-round teaching, block scheduling, increased paperwork, school violence, and student drug abuse will also make teaching far more difficult in terms of the expenditure of energy and time effort by classroom teachers. An expanded, more social-service type of time-intensive role for the classroom teacher might emerge and add to the increasing time burdens of the teacher. *The school organization of the future might also be far more market driven than tradition driven, and the cyclical time clock, common in past eras of public education, might be replaced by the modern linear time clock, common to most consumer-driven service organizations.*

In a more free agent, open, technology-oriented, and competitive type of school organization, teachers might actually have to lose some control over their time, in and out of the classroom, to even have a job. The loss of time control by classroom teachers has already happened in some charter and magnet school programs because they have more of a free market orientation. In these schools, many older teachers who do not participate in the program with their time are asked to leave and teach elsewhere. These teachers are easily replaced by teachers with no competing time-consuming activities in their lives. These time-free or less time-constrained teachers are more time giving and willing to make the needed time commitment.

The world of the school organization typically has a view of time and objectives for the use of time that is quite different from, and in many cases opposite to, that of the typical classroom teacher (see Table 4.1).

Outside private businesses and legislative organizations that tend to run on a linear time clock have naturally become the strongest proponents for school reform and change. These entities also want the pace of time or the clocks between school organizations and other work organizations in the economy to be similar. Because of the linear nature of time in private work organizations, a different set of time incentives for their employees results. If time is not invested by the individual working in the private sector organization, then there is simply no job. These differences in time structures—linear versus cyclical—are the primary reasons why reform and change is so much easier in private business organizations than in school organizations. So although it is easy for school reformers to blame classroom teachers for the slow pace of school change and reform, teachers are not totally at fault.

The question of exactly what is needed in the way of school organizations' reform and change will, in many instances, be aligned to one's personal experience or professional memory in the classroom. A major challenge for educational leaders, therefore, is to develop and articulate, clearly and unambiguously, why the school reform effort is truly worth the time effort of all teachers—young, middle aged, and older. The burden of proof lies not with the teacher, but with the educational leaders of the school organization.

Teachers who have been in the classroom for more than 20 years have seen (or are familiar with), over their careers, many of the currently proposed school and instructional reforms. *These teachers might therefore be naturally skeptical of the "newer" reform proposals producing anything of worth to the education of children.* With their memory of past failures, these teachers might conclude that the reform effort is not worth their participation. Teachers, especially those who remember past reform failures, are placed in a difficult position of being critics of the reform and change process because they have "seen versions of the reform before and it didn't work" in their classroom. The experience and memories of these classroom teachers are invaluable to school reform and change efforts because they know what has to be changed or modified in the proposed reforms to make them work in the classroom.

**TABLE 4.1** A School Organization's World of Time

| | |
|---|---|
| The school clock-cyclical time frame for: | |
| *Evolving and changing* | Infinite amount of time-repetitive tasks over time; no set beginning, no set end, defined interval |
| *School resource input to the process* | Teachers, facilities, dollars, parents, student time |
| *Societal legitimacy and visibility as a goal for schools* | Pursuit of recognition, validation, and social support |
| *School outputs—productive criteria for participation* | Cognitive, affective, and psychosocial student development |

Of all the modern school reforms that have been suggested by legislative bodies, the reform that seems to have made the most inroads in the school organizational setting is the adoption and incorporation of computer technology in the classroom. The fact that there were large corporate gifts of computers and extreme pressure came from these industries to adopt computer technology to classroom use certainly helped accelerate this reform effort into the classroom setting—regardless of teacher support.

Unfortunately, there is an important time problem associated with a technology-oriented school reform that should be considered. Classroom teachers have to make a massive time investment in a technology that is itself rapidly changing. Every 5 or 6 years additional time investments then have to be made by these same classroom teachers in a newer technology to replace the older technology. Technology-based reforms thus set up a revolving door for change before instructional benefits for the classroom teacher can be realized.

What is suggested in this analysis is that many school reform efforts have a short half-life (the time it takes for the reform to become outdated), whereas other school reforms have a very long half-life. Short half-life school reforms tend to lower the satisfaction to time effort ($S/TE$) ratio for classroom teachers because the time investments by classroom teachers have to be made on a continual basis throughout their teaching careers. The constant pace of technological change, plus the unfulfilled promises of classroom benefits promised by earlier technology-based reforms, places the reform at risk of not being worth the extra time effort for the average classroom teacher.

When there is school organizational uncertainty regarding the formal and informal time expectations of teachers to service the needs for school reform, then time investment ambiguity results. With time investment ambiguity there is a tendency for classroom teachers to do their own thing with their own time. When school organizations require that teachers invest large amounts of their personal or extra noncontract time in time-consuming activities that run counter to their individual lifestyle needs or time-efficient teaching practices, then time investment conflict results. Both types of situations (time investment ambiguity and conflict) eventually become counterproductive to school reform and change efforts, because they lower teacher morale by raising time effort and lowering satisfaction. When a school organization requires too much time from its classroom teachers, a sense of time investment overload results. The sense of time investment overload can then lead to stress, burnout, pushout, and dropout. Classroom teachers working in school organizations that have conditions of time investment overload, time investment conflict, and time investment ambiguity become "time stressed." Time stress then becomes a major precursor to anti-school reform and change behaviors. *In essence, dissension and most opposition by classroom teachers toward a specific school reform effort generally have time investment conflict, time investment ambiguity, and time investment overload as underlying causes.*

School organizations exercise control over formal teacher-student contact by use of class schedules, rates of normal progress, and career paths for teachers. The "where" of a student-related time-consuming activity (schedules and calendars), the "rate" or normal progress and the frequency of activities (number of times an activity is needed and time expectation with regard to curriculum delivery), and the "sequencing" of activities (how activities are linked in time to each other or grade-to-grade articulation) are typically used by the school organization to maximize their goals of efficiency, social legitimacy, and visibility.

Unfortunately, other social organizations and special interest groups also want to be a part of formal student contact time. This places more time demands on the classroom teacher and contributes to curriculum-time compression. For example, parent groups, professional associations, and teacher unions can sometimes make additional classroom time demands on teachers via their political actions in the community. Some of these additional time demands are listed in Table 4.2.

Because new instructional strategies, updated curriculums, and technological innovations are highly information based, some school reform efforts require a conscious effort on the part of individual classroom teachers to invest time out of their lifetime (usually at home) to seek this information. The added investment of time that school organizations require from teachers outside of the school setting, or "keeping up" time, is another time burden that many teachers resist. Because some student achievement benefits and other organizational legitimacy goals are long term, many classroom teachers don't expect to be in the school organization when the "pay-off" time occurs. For these older teachers, outside-of-school time investments are essentially nonrecoverable in terms of their personal benefits. In short, for older teachers, school reform efforts entail extra time effort with little or no anticipated benefit or satisfaction.

*Because teachers cannot create more time, they are left with making important time investment choices: taking time from other time-consuming activities in their lifetime or making more efficient use of the time they use in the school organization.* In an attempt to find more time in the day, one of the major movements promoted by educational leaders and school reformers is to develop and support time-management and time-efficiency skills for classroom teachers.

The time management movement has made enormous inroads into both the philosophy and management of the school organizations. Time management proposes a sort of time "alchemy" of changing nonproductive classroom teacher time into productive time for the school organization. Attempting to get more hours out of the workday is similar to the alchemist's dream of changing lead to gold, and school organizations hope to tap into this newfound teacher time. What seems to be happening with this newfound time, however, is that time released to teachers does not result in more time for the school organization, but more time for the teacher to invest and pursue activities directed at increasing lifestyle satisfaction: more time to exercise, be with family, moonlight, and develop hobbies. Attempts at getting more time for school reform efforts by

**TABLE 4.2** Exogenous Forces Demanding More Direct Student
Contact Time in the Classroom and as Part of the
Curricula

| | |
|---|---|
| AIDS awareness | Social behavior groups |
| Drug prevention | Values or character education |
| Gender studies | Ecology |
| Diversity studies | Sex education |
| Conflict resolution | Community service learning |

instituting longer school days and a longer school year have been
generally unsuccessful because these efforts are not economically
viable or financially acceptable to teachers. Teachers tend to resist
longer school days and a longer school year because they conflict
with the other activities in their personal lives.

The time management movement is, of course, a natural extension of scientific management. The mentality of the time management movement is that time efficiency should be reviewed in the
workplace in efforts of generating greater productivity from workers. Similar to time-motion studies of work and assembly lines, time
management discounts all other types of time engagement—especially other- and inner-directed time. Instead, time management focuses complete attention on outer-directed (materially directed)
time in the school organization. For teachers with varied time-
intensive interests and talents, school organizational emphasis on
time management is usually not too productive because teachers require these other uses of time (other- and inner-directed time) to re-
vitalize their "spirit" as classroom teachers.

Regarding the notion of time choice, organizations prioritize
their time expectations in a manner similar to individual teachers
(see discussion in previous chapter).

*Critical—a crisis: Must do.* Here there is simply no choice, and
constraints on both needed time investments and needed fiscal resources are removed to see the project through to fruition. For example, an accreditation report that must be completed by a certain date
requires maximum teacher time and school resource commitment.
Time and fiscal resources are then taken from other time-consuming
activities in the school organization to meet this need.

*Important, but not critical: Should do.* Here, within school organizational resource constraints, time is demanded of teachers to meet certain deadlines. For example, in preparing for statewide testing, teachers use classroom time. Time is, therefore, taken from other activities to meet this need, but no new additional resources are provided by the school organization.

*Normal functioning: Can do.* Within both time and resource constraints, new ideas and proposals are developed. Neither time nor resources are taken from other time-consuming activities to meet this need. Instead, time is added on to the workload on a volunteer basis. For example, teachers interested in gender equity or assessment reform would meet on their own time to discuss these issues. This uncompensated extra time is taken from the lifetimes of teachers and, of course, a major selection bias results between those teachers who can and those who cannot provide the time.

Naturally, convincing all classroom teachers that certain activities in the school organization are critical or important is a major aspect of effective educational leadership in an era of time scarcity.

In conclusion, the school organizational search for productivity and legitimacy has led to the precise definition of time and time use for its classroom teachers. In an effort to lessen time investment conflict, time investment, ambiguity, and time investment overload, lesson plans, class schedules, and salary schedules have emerged in the school organization. Two of these formal strategies for controlling teachers' time are the class schedule and school calendar (see Table 4.3).

## Structuring Teacher Time in School Organizations

The centripetal force that pulls teachers to invest their time in activities within the school organization and the centrifugal force that pulls teachers to invest their time in activities outside of the school organization have both economic and psychological consequences for the classroom teacher. To deal with these time investment conflict problems or professional and personal time investments, school organizations impose time-structuring strategies such as lesson plans, class schedules, school calendars, and career paths.

**TABLE 4.3** Structuring Time for Teachers

| | |
|---|---|
| Schedule | Usually on a daily basis, the class schedule depicts how hours are arranged in the school day. The schedule affects the lifetimes of teachers and includes school reforms and modifications such as modular scheduling, block scheduling, and extended-day programs. |
| School calendar | The school calendar, how days and weeks are organized during the school year, affects the lifetimes of teachers and includes school reform and modifications such as the extended school year calendar, year-round schooling, and dual-session schooling. |

*The purpose of these formal time investment strategies is to get teacher time and school organizational time coordinated with each other and to lessen time investment ambiguity and time investment conflict.* Note how minutes, hours, weeks, years, and even decades of a classroom teacher can be formally influenced by school organizational policies with regard to time (see Table 4.4).

### The Lesson Plan (Controlling Teacher Time to the Minute)

The traditional purpose of requiring lesson plans by classroom teachers in school organizations was to account for and structure the minutes of time in the day. Time used by classroom teachers in a classroom setting was thus formally accounted for by the school organization. In school organizations with a strong teacher union and professional associations, the requirement of written lesson plans by teachers has largely been eliminated. School organizations that would require lesson plans for each class for each day for each year would certainly result in lower teacher satisfaction with teaching and greatly increase their time effort in the classroom. The resulting lowered *S/TE* ratio would then lead to widespread resentment by teachers and to dropout, burnout, and massive turnovers in instructional staff. Today, even though formal class time is set by the school organization, what is done or how time is allocated to various instructional efforts in the classroom is largely left

**TABLE 4.4** Organizational Control of Teacher Time

| *School Organizational Strategy With Regard to Time* | *Scope of Time Control* |
| --- | --- |
| Lesson plans | Minutes |
| Schedules of classes | Hours |
| Specific calendar events | Weeks |
| School calendars | Year |
| Career paths | Decades |

to the teacher. *The isolation of the classroom teacher and subject matter specialties permit a sense of time control over work that is not found in other work organizations.*

The formal linking of teacher instructional time in the classroom with the behavioral instructional objectives associated with student learning led to the development of lesson plans and measurement-driven instruction school reforms. Interestingly, research into teacher proof curricula, measurement-driven instruction, and the use of instructional technologies to deliver instruction are attempts at a revision back to a minute-by-minute formal time control over the classroom teacher by the school organization.

Some teachers have responded to the lesson-plan type of time control strategy imposed by the school organization by investing their time and developing their lesson plans in the early phases of their career in the classroom. These teachers would then use these same lesson plans for the rest of their career in the classroom in an effort to recoup this large initial time investment. School organizations, therefore, might indirectly contribute to the problem of teacher stagnation by creating a time investment incentive system for teachers to make large, early-career time investments in teaching, then in late career use the same lesson plans to recoup their time investment. In essence, teacher stagnation might be a natural consequence of the lesson plan policy or school organizational policies that ensure teacher "ownership" of the classroom setting or a subject matter area. *Because a teacher is permitted to teach the same class, year after year, and in a cyclical time frame, the school organization can contribute to the problem of classroom teacher stagnation.*

### The Schedule (by the Hour) and
### the School Calendar (by the Week and Year)

The purpose of a daily class school schedule is to ensure that teachers and students meet at some prescribed point and place in time to deliver and receive the instructional program. Regardless of individual teacher time needs or the time needs of the teacher outside of the classroom, the school organization sets the clock (in hours) for each teacher to meet with students and to formally meet student contractual obligations. If teachers cannot meet this specified time requirement, then they can take a formal absence day or a personal leave day, and a substitute teacher can be provided. The liberal personal leave and school absentee policies of many schools permit teachers to adapt classroom schedule time needs to their own personal time needs outside of the classroom. By "taking" time from the school organization, classroom teachers have an opportunity to adapt to their personal (the self) and professional (the persona) time needs. Block schedules, traditional schedules, and modular schedules are also attempts by school organizations to formally modify teacher time within the time structure of the school organization. Some of these school calendar efforts have met with widespread teacher opposition because they require major changes in instructional delivery, thus requiring more time effort.

Frequently, when concerns over poor student academic attainment in the school organization are brought to the attention of the public, demands for increased time for instruction during the academic school year result in changes in school programs, extended school day, extended school year, and other modifications to the traditional school calendar. To support these school calendar reform efforts, comparisons are usually made with the length of the school year in other countries such as China, Japan, Israel, and Great Britain. Powerful arguments are then made to bring the United States up to world-class standards with regard to formal instructional time. Changing class time schedules, along with associated changes in the length of the school year, however, has significant time implications for the classroom teacher. Calendar changes are usually met with strong opposition because either elapsed time (longer school year) or high time efforts (longer class periods for classroom teachers) are implied. For example, the time effort for an older teacher to teach a 90-minute instructional block might possibly be much higher and far more physically strenuous than that for a younger teacher. Naturally, lesson plans developed by classroom teachers for traditional instructional block schedules would have to be completely changed or modified to accommodate the needs of the modified, longer teaching block. The tendency for teachers not equipped or trained to teach in longer instructional time blocks is to develop "filling time" activities in the classroom for students in order to increase the $S/TE$ ratio. Instructional activities that were worth the students' time in the traditional setting might then be replaced with time-filling activities in the modified setting such as surfing the Internet. With the entertainment-oriented, filling-time characteristics of computer games, the Internet, and the mass media, larger blocks of class time and school calendar reform might actually hinder classroom learning by permitting more filler and nondirect classroom time. In essence, even though these students might have more instructional time on paper (quantitative) in the academic year, with a modified calendar what may actually be delivered to them in the classroom might be the same or less (qualitative) because of the large amounts of filling-time activities rather than directed time-consuming instructional activities. The school reform as designed by educational leaders might be quite different from the school reform as delivered in the classroom by the teacher. This discrepancy in reforms-as-designed versus reforms-as-delivered is a result of classroom teachers' adjustment of the $S/TE$ ratio.

Because school calendar reform has both potential benefits and liabilities for the classroom teacher, these types of reforms must be carefully engineered into the school organization. One way to engineer school calendar reform is to explicitly consider the $S/TE$ ratio for the classroom teacher and find ways to both increase satisfaction ($S$) and lower time effort ($TE$). For example, traditional fixed blocks of instruction have the advantage of short, intense lessons (lower $TE$), whereas longer blocks of instructional time create more of an opportunity to individualize instruction (higher $S$). School calendar reform, changing daily teaching schedules, extending the instruction day, and extending the academic school year are typically opposed by classroom teachers because many teachers plan their lives, lessons, and activities around the traditional fixed-block class schedule and thus have reached a steady state $S/TE$ ratio. If the calendar reform can add to the salary of classroom teachers, then many teachers, especially younger teachers, would support the reform because $S$ would be increased through material compensation.

Historically, school calendar reform efforts began in the early 1960s with the introduction of a modular system of class scheduling. Modular scheduling proved to be somewhat ineffectual in the classroom because many students used the extra class time provided by the reform for doing "independent" study, thus lowering the $TE$ of the classroom teacher. Research of this time period revealed that without a fixed classroom schedule, some students got lost in the shuffle and did not take full advantage of the increased instructional time that was made available by the school calendar reform.

In short, reforms that are aimed at class schedule and school calendar modifications require teachers to make substantial investments of their own personal time in order to modify their approaches to teaching. Schools also have to make huge time investments in their staff development program to develop new teaching practices and instructional methods to take full advantage of the extra classroom time. Finally, more in-depth curriculums and more active student engagement require more time from teachers for planning lessons as well as teaching.

As one teacher in the study noted,[1]

> I had to create two different tests that would equally assess my students that were taking the same class but now on different days. I had to learn how to create lesson plans for twice the amount of class time. However, I am not against block scheduling. I was a strong proponent of it. Change takes time and that the new schedule be eliminated, just because it did not work well for all the teachers, is wrong. All new ways of teaching have their flaws, but I really think that block scheduling would work well for all involved.

A major type of school calendar reform has to do with the academic year itself. Some teachers prefer the traditional 4-month break in the school year, other teachers prefer two 2-month breaks during the school year. There are powerful and persuasive arguments for the traditional as well as yearly calendars, so the school calendar issue really boils down to personal teacher preference, the $S/TE$ ratio, and the potential for alternative investments of time in the lifetime of a classroom teacher.

The year-round school format has become an extremely controversial school reform precisely because it tends to interfere with the yearly personal time plans of teachers. Older teachers and teachers with families who are used to (and planned their lives around) traditional calendars would have to adjust their lives and personal schedules to go to a year-round format. College and university programs for teachers would also have to be modified. It would certainly be advantageous if all schools in the county agreed to one school calendar. Great stress in the lives of classroom teachers results when two-income homes with children, all on different school year calendars, try to coordinate time schedules for common family activities. In fact, difficulties encountered in adapting to year-round school calendars have forced many parents to enroll their children in private schools that are on traditional school calendars.

Arguably, the traditional school calendar has provided teachers with a large block of time for a much-needed rejuvenation period. A year-round school provides two or more smaller teacher rejuvenation periods. However, because of needed extra salary, many teachers prefer to teach during their intersession time period at a traditional summer school, thus making the exhausting task of teaching a full-time, 12-month job. Research is still pending, but it would not be too surprising to discover that older teachers tend to favor the traditional school calendar, simply because their recovery from school-related activities takes longer and their lives are planned around traditional school calendars. Younger teachers, usually with no time-consuming family activities, on the other hand, might want shorter and more frequent breaks from schooling activities, because their recovery is faster and they can enjoy the breaks in the program with recreational interests, travel, or hobbies. Younger teachers with families might also use this vacation time to moonlight either in the school organization by teaching during this intersession or outside the school organization with real estate or other jobs in the community.

One teacher in the study nicely summarized the pros and cons of traditional versus year-round schools:

I am finishing my third year of teaching at a traditional school, and I am moving to a year-round in July. I feel that traditional schools are still best for students, but I prefer the year-round schedule. The kids benefit from traditional schooling in two ways: (1) They need a sufficient vacation to recharge their batteries, and (2) they need that significant break to signify their passage from grade to grade. It does not work as well if a fourth grader is a fifth grader after a 2-week break. As the teacher, though, I have the ability to earn extra money, as it is easier to pick up off-track hours than summer school in a traditional setting. Personally, I do not like the length of an entire summer vacation. The first few weeks after summer vacation were usually a waste, and it took too long for me to get back in the teaching groove.

In short, changes in school year calendars will always be extremely controversial, not primarily because of their effects on students academically, but because they attempt to control the yearly time behaviors of teachers and thus affect the *S/TE* ratio of teaching.

Adding to the time demands of teachers involved with classroom instruction are a whole set of "volunteer" or poorly paid extra events in the school year that repeat themselves each year. For many teachers, these yearly events in the school calendar, such as state testing, proms, yearbooks, and school sports, are the straws that break the camel's back. The month of May is particularly time compressed with a multitude of time-consuming events and activities. The end of the academic school year, therefore, is not the best time to ask teachers to cooperate and participate in the extra time-consuming activities that are associated with school reform and change.

---

One of the major accomplishments of teacher unions in recent decades is lessening the amount of free or uncompensated time that teachers have to provide to the school organization.

---

If teachers are formally held by the school organization to their time commitments and must account for each minute of their time, then the willingness of teachers to commit their free time to these yearly school activities might be challenged, especially by teacher unions. In fact, one of the major accomplishments of teacher unions in recent decades is lessening the amount of free or uncompensated time that teachers have to provide to the school organization. If educational leaders become too rigid with teacher time accountability, then teachers have the option to "pull the plug" on the time efforts that they presently volunteer to a school organization. It is potentially a lose-lose situation for both the classroom teacher and the school organization.

## Career Paths (by Decades)

School organizations directly and formally govern the time associated with career paths of individual teachers through their incentive or compensation systems. In most school organizations, the preferred and most common method for salary compensation is the fixed-step salary schedule. In the fixed-step salary schedule, a teacher's salary is based on two factors: highest degree and teaching experience. Time investment for change and reform or the extra time needed by the school organization from classroom teachers is usually not financially compensated by the salary schedule.

Ostensibly, a teacher giving the minimum amount of extra participation time to the school and a teacher who gives enormous amounts of after-school participation time—with the same degree and college units and experience—would be paid at the same salary level.

These salary schedules nicely depict how an organization classifies, creates incentives, and rewards the work life of classroom teachers over their career in the school organization. Although there is little or any statistical relationship between the two salary compensation factors of experience and highest academic degree plus college credits to the quality of classroom teaching, the fixed-step salary schedule is simple to communicate and objective to evaluate. It simply rewards classroom teachers who put in the time to the school organization, but says nothing about the quality of this time and amount of extra time provided for planning school reforms and change.

Another time-oriented part of the compensation package for teachers that is traditionally provided by the school organization is sabbatical leave, sick (absentee) leave, and unpaid personal leave. In some areas of the country, policies on sabbatical leave from the classroom have been abandoned or drastically curtailed. In some school organizations, particularly universities, sabbatical leave is granted only if there is no additional cost to the school organization, that is, if the job function is covered by other personnel. Personal leave and sick leave are many times accumulated by teachers and then taken as one set amount of leave at retirement. Although illegal, sometimes personal leave time is used for purposes of moonlighting because many teachers consider personal leave to be a time benefit provided by the school organization.

If school organizations were static and were not required to use teacher time to invest in the change or reform process, then school organizational and classroom teacher individual time interests could easily be coordinated. *Unfortunately, the compression of school curricula where more and more information has to be taught in less and less time, the increasing demands of social and cultural diversity, and the increasing role of advanced technologies in classroom instruction will require that teachers make larger periodic investments of time in their own "teaching capital" at several junctures throughout the course of their teaching careers.* Thus, besides the actual time "sold" to the school organization to service direct classroom teaching functions during school hours (contract time), additional extra time at school has to be invested beyond the classroom to accommodate the changing context of teaching.

Other time-consuming activities are those that relate to employment as classroom teachers but do not take place during their formal class time at school. An example of this type of associated time is the parent-teacher conference, which in the past has occurred after school but now frequently occurs during school hours. After-school time tends to divide into the categories of time needed to assist children, time needed in class preparation, time needed to keep up with the profession, time for staff meetings and ad hoc committees, and time needed for union and professional obligations.

As one teacher noted with regard to staying after school,

I am a teacher and, like any other employee, I punch a clock and just come in for what is required of me. It is not just staying after school. I have xeroxing to do, test making to do, reviewing to do. There are lots of things I have to do. Some of them are involved in extracurricular activities.

The amount of teaching experience that a teacher has in the classroom appears to affect the amount of after-school extra time provided to the school organization. One teacher contrasts his several years of teaching experience with that of his wife, who has been teaching for only 1 year:

> There is a real difference between new teachers and old teachers. My wife . . . is doing work all the time. She has no time. She is grading papers, setting up her new class. I have been teaching a lot longer, so I don't have to prepare quite so much.

## Summary

Unlike the classroom teacher who requires time to develop the persona as a teacher and to find the self, the school organization uses time as a currency to ensure its successful evolution, productivity, competitiveness, legitimacy, and visibility in society. Whereas the school organization looks at time importance, the classroom teacher looks at time worth. To control a teacher's time in the school organization, reduce time investment conflict, lessen time investment ambiguity, and address the issue of time investment overload, educational leaders rely on time structures such as lesson plans, daily class schedules, yearly events, school calendars, and career paths. Each of these time-oriented strategies affects the lifetime of a teacher by lessening the nonpecuniary benefit of time control on the part of the teacher. Any attempt by educational leaders to change the locus of control over time can be counted on to generate widespread conflict and dissatisfaction among classroom teachers.

---

Unless time factors are explicitly considered by school leaders, there will be wide discrepancies between school reforms as designed and school reforms as delivered to the classroom.

---

Simply put, school reforms and change efforts have to be economically viable in time, financially feasible in time, maintainable in time, and politically acceptable in time for them to have a lasting impact on the school organization. A breakdown in any one of these criteria will lead to a short-lived school reform effort and generate a memory of failure that will be imparted to the next generation of teachers. More important, unless these time factors are explicitly considered by school leaders, there will be wide discrepancies between school reforms as designed by leaders in the school organization and school reforms as delivered by classroom teachers in the classroom.

## Perspectives, Points of View, Discussion

- What are some of the ways that school organizations control the time of their teachers?
- Is it possible to change the way teachers are compensated in order to take into account their time investments in the school organization and to promote school change and reform?
- Do you think that technological innovations and the use of technology in instruction will change the time relationships between the classroom teacher and the school organization?
- Do you feel that modern school calendar reform, that is, year-round schools, will significantly affect the clock of the school organization and the classroom teacher?
- How would you view and reward loyalty of classroom teachers from a time perspective, and is classroom teacher loyalty important for the school organization?

## NOTE

1. This quote and other quotes in this chapter, unless otherwise noted, are from personal interviews with teachers.

# 5

# Bridging Teacher Time and School Time: Pulling Together

*Time is dead as long as it is being clicked off by little wheels; only when the clock stops does time come to life.*

WILLIAM FAULKNER
(*THE SOUND AND THE FURY*, 1929)

---

- Pulling Together in Time: Linking Teacher Time With School Time
- Congruence and Conflicts in Time: Organizational Time Demands Versus Teacher Time Needs
- Commitment or Burnout: Exchanges Between Teacher Time and School Time
- Summary
- Perspectives, Points of View, Discussion

---

### Pulling Together in Time: Linking Teacher Time With School Time

Similar to the harmony and coordination of effort displayed by a fine symphony orchestra, "pulling together" is a concept that implies time coordination in the workplace. Can classroom teachers be placed on the same time clock as the school organization? Can school leaders, like symphony orchestra conductors, coordinate classroom teachers' efforts with their own to produce the required school changes and reforms? Teachers at different ages and at different instructional levels, and teaching different subject matter areas, make any attempt at teacher-organizational time coordination in school organizations particularly challenging for educational leaders. Unfortunately, *school reform and change efforts become impeded when teachers are paced by a different clock than that of the school organization.* The speed of implementation of school reforms, therefore, greatly depends on the degree to which school leaders can get teachers to pull together in time in the school organization. Reform and change, more often than not, are oriented toward the slowest changing teacher rather than the fastest changing teacher. It is important, therefore, that the concept of currency of time exchanges between the school organization and the classroom teacher be appreciated and understood by school leaders before embarking on any school reform and change effort.

---

The pushed-out teacher, or the teacher who wants to participate in reform activities but does not have the time, might be of far greater importance to the school reform movement than the marginal teacher who has the time to participate. The memory of older teachers and the vision of younger teachers are both needed for school reform to attain its intended goals of school improvement to support learning.

---

Previous chapters examined how teachers and school organizations with linear and cyclical time perspectives use and interact with the psychosocial construct of time to attain their individual self-actualization and organizational evolution goals. Three methods that school organizations use to coordinate time with classroom teachers were discussed: (a) reductions in time investment uncertainty and time investment ambiguity through class and yearly schedules, (b) resolution of time investment conflicts between teachers and the school organizations through school calendars, and (c) ensuring against time investment overload for teachers while attempting to create incentives for teachers to invest their "extra" time in the school organization.

The following are some of the relationships between teacher time needs and school organization time needs that will be discussed in this chapter.

• Aging teachers in school organizations have a different sense of time passage and time urgency because the ratio of time lived to time remaining gets larger. Each hour of time for an older classroom teacher, therefore, has a higher subjective worth or weight than an hour of time for a younger teacher. These differences in subjective weighted hours lead to major differences in observed time investment behaviors between classroom teachers in school reform activities.

• Traditionally, teachers and school organizations formed professional associations to promote their common goals, and both freely gave and invested their time to attain these goals. With the emergence of teacher unions, major conflicts arose over who was to be in control of a teacher's time—the teacher, the school organization, or the teacher union. Conflicts between teachers and school organizations, therefore, have a large component based on time investment and time control. Failure to correct these time conflicts typically results in teacher observed behaviors of dropout, burnout, and pushout.

• The self-worth of classroom teachers is directly related to the value placed on their time by the school organization. Not paying, or not rewarding with praise and recognition, classroom teachers for their time investments results in resentment toward the school organization. By devaluing teacher time or minimizing the worth of teacher time, a "pay for services rendered" type of work attitude on the part of classroom teachers prevails.

• Happy teachers are important to the school reform and change process because they teach their "selves" to their students. Happy and productive teachers are in control of their time in their lifetimes, like what they do, like children, and are accomplishing their personal goals of lifestyle satisfaction. This type of happy, goal-attaining teacher is far more important for promoting classroom learning than any school reform effort.

• Classroom teachers are extraordinarily different with regard to their perceptions of time and the time investments they are willing to give or "sell" to the school organization. Gender, race, age, instructional level, and subject matter affect the teacher's perception and investments of time in the school organization.

• Loyalty on the part of teachers to educational leaders and loyalty by educational leaders to classroom teachers are an important component to successful school reform. Loyalty or trust can only be built over long periods of time. Unfortunately, it takes only seconds to destroy trust by politically oriented and time-insensitive educational leaders.

• Educational leaders need to view teacher compensation for their extra time investments from a broader perspective to include not only material rewards but also, of even greater importance for older teachers, social, psychological, and personal professional development compensation.

• Getting teachers to participate in the multitude of extra time-consuming activities of the school organizations requires that educational leaders consider the satisfaction to time effort ($S/TE$) ratio of the activity as an important predictor and a measure of participation attractiveness. Efforts, therefore, have to be made by school leaders to increase classroom teacher satisfaction and lower their time effort for the school reform activity.

This chapter examines in more detail some of the important linkages between the linear time frame perspective of the classroom teacher and the cyclical time frame perspective of the school organization. Using this broader perspective, time can be viewed as a currency of exchange between the individual teacher who ages under a linear time frame with a finite amount of time in a lifetime and the school organization that evolves under a cyclical time frame with a virtually infinite amount of time in a life span.

The intersection of the world of the school organization and the world of the classroom teacher in many instances produces serious

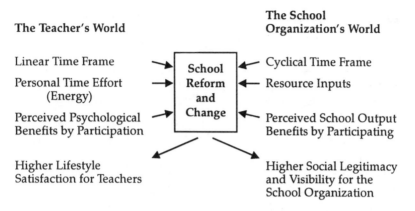

**Figure 5.1.** Bridging the Teacher's World and the School Organization's World

conflict with regard to needed time investments because the purposes or objectives are different and both are operating under different time clocks (see Figure 5.1).

Using the currency of time perspective (see Table 5.1), both the teacher and the school organization can either lose or gain from the exchange of time sold or given by the classroom teacher to the school organization. The time "bought" or appropriated by the school organization from classroom teachers is equally important. For a classroom teacher, the downside aspects of time and aging in the school organization are the midlife crisis and the propensity to drop out, be pushed out, be plateaued, and to burnout from classroom teaching. In essence, the compensation objectives and the consequences of time exchanges between classroom teachers and school organizations result in classroom behaviors such as those described in Table 5.1.

In the research literature, time-sensitive, adaptive behaviors of adults have been explored in many important psychological works (Colarusso, 1994; Nemiroff & Colarusso, 1985) and organizational studies (Bardwick, 1986). The linkages between the time structures of the work organization and the time structures of the individual have also been explored in the research of Hassard (1991) and Howard and Bray (1988). Finally, teacher time commitments in the school organization have been referenced in the works of Fullan and Miles (1992), Hannaway and Carnoy (1993), Johansen (1992), and Milstein

**TABLE 5.1** Time as the Currency of Exchange

| School Organization Time | Individual Teacher Time |
|---|---|
| **Compensation goals and objectives** | **Compensation goals and objectives** |
| Legitimacy, visibility, and status | Selling time = Material compensa- |
| Social service | tion |
| | Giving time = Social compensation |
| | Spending time = Personal compen- |
| | sation |
| | Filling time = Filling of emptiness |

← Currency of exchange (time) →

| Consequences of Failure to Fulfill Goals and Objectives | Consequences of Failure to Fulfill Goals and Objectives |
|---|---|
| Abandonment | Dropout |
| Commitment | Commitment |
| Low priority | Burnout |
| Replacement | Pushout |
| State takeover of control of schools | Marking time |
| | Plateaued |

(1990a, 1990b). Specific references to the time structures of teachers and the school organization have appeared in the works of Ben-Peretz and Bromme (1990), Hargraves (1992), and McGrath and Rotchford (1983).

The leadership challenges associated with the linkage between teacher time and the school reform movement are extremely important to appreciate: "Time has emerged as the key issues in every analysis of school change appearing in the last decade" (Raywid, 1993, p. 30). Because school organizations have such a profound impact on shaping the temporal experience of the classroom teacher, understanding the linkage between time and teacher behavior in the classroom has to be viewed as being an extremely important part of school leadership.

In studies of school organizations, there are many different types of teaching personas built over time that can be used to describe a classroom teacher's time interaction with the school organization. Using the principle of time directedness, the persona of a classroom teacher can be described in terms of time investments and the $S/TE$ ratio for various time-consuming activities. The following are typical comments from an outer-directed or organization-centered teacher (materially oriented and compensated):[1]

I always wanted more time for my kids. At one point in my life I couldn't get enough work [selling time], then when kids arrived I wanted to be with my family. Later in life as my kids left home, I refocused energies and put in 12- to 15-hour workdays because of the motivating factor of promoting my project at school, a project for personal reasons that I wanted to succeed.

Compare the comments of the above outer-directed teacher with the interactions of an other-directed or student-directed (social relationship compensation) teacher:

I was tired of fighting battles with bureaucratic red tape so I left the mainstream public school and began teaching at an alternative school where the pace of the clock was more in my control and I could get to know my students.

Finally, compare the comments of both the outer- and other-directed teachers with the school organizational interactions of an inner- or self-directed (psychological compensation) teacher:

I spend enormous amounts of time working with my hobby of stamp collecting, and I use many of these ideas for lessons in history and geography.

For classroom teachers, time is an important element in the Faustian type of bargain where time is exchanged for material, social, or personal professional development rewards in life. Because classroom teachers can "get by" in school organizations by investing their time at minimal levels or go way beyond the minimum time needed because of a sense of professional obligation, extra time investments by teachers in school organizations are highly contextual and can relate to a host of psychosocial factors. The most notable of these factors is the availability or the lack of availability of competing time-consuming activities in the teacher's life, especially if these activities have a higher $S/TE$ ratio.

Teacher-school organizational discord often results when the time investment priorities of the school organizations are at odds with the time investment priorities of the individual teacher. Changes in time investment patterns from defining the persona as a classroom teacher to finding of the self can create turmoil and time conflicts within a teacher's life. *A career plateau or time "armistice," in many instances, is reached between the classroom teacher and the school organization at middle age. At this juncture in a career, many teachers seek other time investments or time-consuming activities that are outside of the school organization and that have a higher S/TE ratio.* Investing time both within and outside of the school organization, therefore, has the same overall objective for the classroom teacher, namely, maximizing lifestyle satisfaction via the attainment of material, social, or personal professional development objectives.

Sometimes a classroom teacher is upwardly mobile and proactive with regard to career advancement. But for reasons outside of his or her control, such as internal economics, politics of the workplace, or the simple lack of availability of leadership and administrative positions, mobility in the school organization is blocked. These teachers tend to become frustrated in the school organization, and because they are blocked or pushed out from further advancement, might become severe critics or dissenters of any school activity requiring extra time effort. For these teachers, the career plateau is not by their choice, but by the choice of the school organization. Thus, although some classroom teachers welcome a career plateau so that they can be psychologically and emotionally free to allocate their time to other time-consuming activities in life, other teachers become alienated from the school organization and feel pushed out.

In private sector organizations, unlike school organizations, time-consuming activities of professionals are associated with earning a living in a highly competitive and constantly changing marketplace. Individuals in these free market organizations thus have to continually adjust their time investments and update their marketable skills to stay competitive and be able to sell their time to the work organization at the market clearing price. Whereas some of these "keeping up" time investments are done at work, for most professionals, such as doctors and lawyers, much of this time investment is done at home and on weekends. These private sector professional must keep up and invest time (primarily their "own" time and at more than the minimum levels required) to even have a job and a future with the organization. It is the open market condition of needed time investment that drives the organization toward change. All employees who work in the organization, therefore, have to march to and be paced by the same time clock as the clock of the organization.

The cyclical-versus-linear time clock is a major time frame perspective difference between schools (cyclical) and private work organizations (linear). In the absence of time investment incentives, it is little wonder that many teachers don't provide or want to give the needed time to participate in any extra time-consuming activities of the school organization. The career habits of classroom teachers formed in school organizations with a cyclical time frame perspective thus become difficult patterns to change, because of the prevailing attitudes: "Why change when it has worked for me as a classroom teacher in the past?" or "Why change when I don't have to change?" or "The proposed change is not worth my time."

Comparing professional employees in a computer industry to teachers in a school organization dramatically underscores these time-laden differences. In the former organization, earning-a-living activities (selling time) on a static information base can be measured in only a few years (half the knowledge becomes outdated), so time from an individual's lifetime has to be continually invested in work to stay competitive and to be able to sell time to an organization that needs their time to stay competitive. In the school organization, the work half-life of many classroom teachers, especially elementary school teachers, can be measured in decades, so there is little need for them to invest extra or additional time to stay competitive. In addition, there is, many times, a vast difference between actual contract time with students in the classroom and the professional "standard of care" time requirements that are needed by the school organization to support the change and reform process.

An interesting scenario to consider would be if two teachers died at the same time, say, in 1975. One classroom teacher taught English literature and the other classroom teacher taught biology. If both of these teachers were resurrected in 1997, the English teacher would probably be able to resume teaching without too much time effort. The biology teacher's knowledge, however, would be hopelessly out of date, and he or she would have to invest a great deal of extra personal time to get to the level where his or her teaching competence would be sufficiently high to be bought by the school organization to again teach biology. In short, the ability to sell one's time in the school organization is highly dependent on time and the rate of decay in the quality of information in the subject matter area. With regard to subject matter half-life and the need to stay current, elementary school teachers thus have a far greater time advantage in the school organization than, say, a high school science or a technology teacher. In fact, many individuals, as undergraduates, have recognized the career half-life characteristic of a profession and have decided to enter the teaching profession precisely because of these career-oriented time characteristics. *In essence, the long career information half-life of being a classroom teacher, especially at the elementary school level, is a major nonpecuniary benefit for most individuals entering the teaching profession.*

In an era of time scarcity, time-oriented school policies toward teachers will eventually distinguish the effective school reform effort from the noneffective school reform effort. Reform effectiveness is the match between the reform as designed by school organizational leaders and the reform that is actually delivered to the students in the classroom by the teacher. As noted earlier, the discrepancy between the design and delivery of a school reform effort is fundamentally a question of time and the degree to which teachers buy into the time demands of the school organization. The difference between school reform design and school reform delivery is also attributable to classroom teachers modifying or adjusting the school reform to lower its time effort ($TE$) and increase its satisfaction ($S$) thus increasing the $S/TE$ ratio in the classroom.

Finally, the most important gift that teachers give to students and to a school organization is time drawn from the finite amount of time in their lifetimes. This gift has to be given by a happy and caring teacher for it to be received in a positive manner by students and the school organization. Unhappy teachers tend to view the teaching act and participation in extra school activities as a "pay per view" type of transaction, and their impact on students and school leaders can be equally cold and ineffective. The fact that many individuals pursue a teaching career precisely because they want to give this time gift to children and the school organization presents a challenge for school leaders to preserve this professional idealism over the career of the classroom teacher.

School organizations have traditionally attempted to extract more time from a classroom teacher's lifetime for designing and planning for school reform by using one or more of the following strategies:

1. Paying teachers extra (but at lower rates) for any extra types of time investment, for example, moonlighting in the district by taking on extra assignments

2. Increasing staff development in the area of time management and technology so that time efficiency would result in more time being available for the school organization

3. Instituting accounting procedures to monitor the elapsed time for certain instructional sequences, then proposing modifications in the class schedule, the school day, or the academic year, to "free up" more classroom teacher time

4. Relying on the professional nature of teachers to want to give extra time (at no additional compensation) to the school organization

5. Instituting a leadership "reign of terror" to coerce teachers to give extra time

6. Agreeing to use contract time for school reform planning and rely on substitute teachers to deliver instruction

7. Having planning and teacher days in the academic school calendar where students are engaged in noninstructional activities and teachers are engaged in school reform activities

Although keeping track of teachers' time needed to perform certain tasks in the school organization might be important for school organizational accounting practices, it is the ratio of $S$ to $TE$ that is important from the perspective of the classroom teacher. In fact, for the "long term" time commitment of a classroom teacher in the school organization, it is extremely important that the $S/TE$ ratio remain high. The $S/TE$ ratio establishes the material, social, and psychological attractiveness of the time-consuming activity. Whereas a narrow, accounting-oriented view of time in instructional minutes might be somewhat useful for the evaluation of the curriculums, time on task, and mastery learning, it might be totally ineffectual for understanding the "why" behind certain types of time-laden classroom teacher behaviors in the school organizations.

Using the principle of psychological "attractiveness" via the $S/TE$ ratio of a time-consuming activity, it should be possible to attract, retain, and stimulate teacher effort in the classroom over the full career of the classroom teacher. Present leadership strategies that ignore this principle and prefer only to attract teachers, use their services for a short time, then remove them when their "time is up" and replace them with another set of teachers are ultimately very harmful for promoting organizational loyalty and classroom learning. This devaluation of loyalty can be devastating to the morale of the teaching staff. The classroom teacher as a "free agent," as in professional sports, is not appropriate to school organizations. Loyalty and traditions are based on time, and loyalty by itself can be a powerful motivator for teachers to want to give extra amounts of their time to the school organization.

---

Time, happiness, and lifestyle satisfaction are all intertwined in the lifetime of a teacher, and teachers, not curriculums, have the most impact on children.

---

In short, if the happy human being we call a teacher wasn't such an important part of a school organization's need to deliver the school curriculum, then the psychological component of a teacher's time would not be important for promoting student learning. Unfortunately, time, happiness, and lifestyle satisfaction are all intertwined in the lifetime of a teacher, and teachers, not curriculums, have the most impact on children. Note some of the time perceptions and characteristics of exchanges between classroom teachers and school organizations found in Table 5.2.

Any school organizational reform that alters this hidden, but extremely important, time component of the teacher-school organization contract is usually met with widespread opposition by classroom teachers. This opposition is especially acute for those teachers who have arrived at their time-effort comfort zone in the school organization and are set in their time-efficient and job-fluent ways. For some classroom teachers, the single greatest nontaxable benefit offered by the school organization is time. It is time that teachers can use to pursue other time-consuming activities in life in their quest for higher levels of lifestyle satisfaction. The implicit psychological contract that is associated with personal control over time is, therefore, extremely important for classroom teachers. The fact that

**TABLE 5.2** Different Concepts of Time Between Teachers and
        School Organizations

| Individual Teachers | School Organization |
| --- | --- |
| Sell | Buy |
| Invest | Consume |
| Life satisfaction | Productivity/legitimacy |
| Linear time | Cyclical time |
| Weighted time | Unweighted time |

teachers are compensated on a fixed-step salary schedule (experience and academic degrees) tends to underscore the fact that, by tradition, the required or contract time investments in the school organization are clearly defined, and extra time investments are ill defined.

### Congruence and Conflicts in Time: Organizational Time Demands Versus Teacher Time Needs

Noncompensated extra time or noncontract time has during the past decades been decreasing for classroom teachers. According to a study by the National Education Association (NEA), the mean number of noncompensated hours spent per week on extra school-related activities from 1966 to 1991 decreased from 10.8 to 8.2 (NEA, 1992, pp. 44-45). From 1966 to 1991, the percentage of teachers who spent between 4 and 16 hours of uncompensated extra school-related time also decreased. In one study of extra time of classroom teachers, 26.5% of the teachers reported spending 10 to 12 weekly hours of extra or uncompensated time in 1966, whereas 21.3% reported doing so in 1991 (NEA, 1992, p. 45). Although there is some evidence of regional variation in the length of the contract, or compensated or required, teacher time, there has been little change in required time during the past several decades. Teachers in the Northeast reported work weeks of 35 or fewer hours and 40 hours or fewer in the West and in the South (NEA, 1992, pp. 44-46).

In April, 1986, one medium-sized school district, after nine months of contract negotiations, reached an impasse over salary increases. Some 550 secondary and elementary school teachers in the school district voted to boycott spring open house evenings, at which parents and teachers have traditionally conferred regarding students. Some teachers also refused to turn in grade reports to school administrators. Instead, teachers planned to stand outside school facilities at the meetings and distribute leaflets explaining the teachers' frustration with the school district. (Braxton, 1986, p. 6)

Issues of teachers' extra time investments beyond formal teaching contract time has resulted in many teacher strikes and union involvement. In May 1989, after 17 months of negotiations and after working for nearly 1 full school year without a contract, teachers in a large urban school district went out on strike for the first time in 19 years. More than two thirds of these teachers were walking picket lines at some point during the work stoppage. Among the most hotly contested issues in the strike were the cancellation of mandatory yard supervision by elementary school instructors and the establishment of teacher participation in school policy administration and development (Enriquez & Gordon, 1989, p. 1). Although elementary school teachers' contracts provided for a 30-minute planning period before school and 10 minutes after class, teachers reported often spending such times on meetings or supervision duties and using lunch periods to do paperwork, plan lessons, use copy machines, or call parents (Woo, 1989, p. 7). The teacher union in this district organized a boycott of all unpaid, extra nonteaching duties such as yard supervision. Some classroom teachers also refused to turn in their end-of-the-year grades as part of the strike (Enriquez & Gordon, 1989, p. 1).

Passive resistance regarding issues of increasing the extra time of classroom teachers has also surfaced in some school districts. In 1990, when contract-renewal negotiations between teachers and another medium-sized school district began to stall, a number of teachers at these schools "stopped assigning homework and refused to participate in extra after-school activities, including open house and faculty meetings" (Marcano, 1990, p. 9).

For older teachers, participating in extra school organizational activities is a time investment that
probably won't pay off in terms of classroom teaching
dividends.

In short, in these and similar disputes around the country, classroom teachers, at the urging of teacher unions, have begun to with-
hold unpaid extra time investments and use this extra or noncontract time as a collective bargaining chip in their negotiations with
school boards. The closer a teacher is to retirement age, the less attractive is participation in the extra time-consuming activities of the
school organization. Linear time frame perspectives of classroom
teachers make time far more valuable and limited in a teacher's lifetime, especially for older teachers, than the cyclical time frame perspectives of the school organization. With the aging process, a profound sense of time scarcity in a classroom teacher develops, and the
sense of time scarcity affects their behavior in the classroom and in
the school organization. In addition, physical progression of an
early career as a classroom teacher is replaced by physical retrogression in the later career in teaching. This retrogression in physical energy tends to automatically increase the time effort for the same
teaching tasks in the school organization. Each unit of time for an
older teacher, therefore, takes on more subjective perceived value or
worth, because the ratio of time lived to time remaining in life becomes larger. Correspondingly, the effort part of the time effort factor also increases for the older teacher because of the physiological
changes that typically occur with age. In essence, time effort for
most classroom teachers, because of these physiological changes,
tends to increase over a career, even if there are no demands for extra time investment by the school organization.

Finally, teachers cannot be expected to reset their linear time career clocks when they are older and act as if time had the same subjective perceived value as when they were younger. *Expecting older
teachers to participate and provide the same time effort to service
school reform and change activities and to have the same attitudes toward the change process as younger teachers is unrealistic and usually
results in ineffectual leadership policies regarding participation and
reform.*

## Commitment or Burnout: Exchanges
## Between Teacher Time and School Time

Given that classroom teachers tend to believe or perceive that they are paying for the cost for school reform and change with time taken from their lifetimes, any reluctance on the part of teachers to provide extra time for school reform and change should be understood by school leaders as being part of the lifespan reality of a classroom teacher. Steps then have to be taken by educational leaders to engineer around the time scarcity problem of classroom teachers by making the activity more materially, socially, or psychologically attractive, that is, increasing satisfaction and at the same time reducing time effort (more instructional support) so that the ratio of both $S$ and $TE$ increase.

In the competition between individual teacher time needs and organizational time demands, teachers are placed at risk of classroom behaviors characterized by pushout, burnout, and dropout. Because school reform efforts, especially those dealing with school site management, require extensive amounts of time for planning, staff development, teacher-administrator-specialist collaboration, training, school site council meetings, and evaluation, many older teachers typically do not wish to participate. Because of their memory and experience in the classroom, however, these veteran teachers could make valuable contributions to the school reform and change debate. Because large numbers of these teachers do not participate in the school reform process, their classroom expertise or memory in the school organization is thus devalued. By extension, the expertise of those teachers who do participate in the reform activity is overvalued.

Unfortunately, by devaluing the memory and expertise of older classroom teachers, school leaders may indirectly undermine the long-term commitment by younger teachers to the school organization because it sends the message that experience doesn't matter. These types of "marginalizing" leadership practices lead to school reform sabotage, anger, and resentment by the excluded teachers. Those who no longer have any loyalty or identification with the school organization become its harshest critics. The hidden cost for devaluing classroom teacher expertise and memory, therefore, could be enormous not only in the obvious area of repeating past mistakes in the school organization and thus wasting time, but also

**TABLE 5.3** Time and Teacher Behaviors in School Organizations

| | |
|---|---|
| Commitment | Teachers fully bond; there is time participation and identification with school organizational goals (leadership) |
| Pushout or marginalization | Teachers view the activity as not worth the time effort investment, but go along (follower) |
| Burnout | Teachers become overworked because time is not made available to accommodate additional classroom workload, while satisfaction remains constant (participation, but at risk) |
| Dropout | Teachers dislike teaching in the school organization both as time effort increases and satisfaction decreases; these teachers begin to moonlight or begin looking for other careers (active dissenter) |

because devaluing institutional memory fosters a "me first" attitude on the part of all teachers. *Future actions and behaviors by these time-devalued teachers become self-serving rather than profession serving, student serving, or organization serving. Paycheck loyalty replaces school organizational loyalty, and eventually replaces professional loyalty.* A vision of a future where the school organization is in partnership with the classroom teacher, a vision where trust and loyalty are common shared virtues, is thus placed at risk as anti-school organizational behavior begins to manifest itself by these time- and experience-devalued teachers.

Teacher-identified behaviors of commitment, pushout, burnout, and dropout (see Table 5.3) are extremely time and loyalty sensitive and can be characterized by behaviors such as commitment to change, opposition to change, minimal commitment, or low priority to change. All of these behaviors are also reflective of the *S/TE* ratio (see Table 5.4).

Given the fact that classroom teachers don't start their teaching career with the intention of becoming burned out, wanting to be a teaching dropout, or becoming negative about participating in school reform and change efforts, then these types of teacher behaviors have to be learned. *If teacher commitment is a desirable, sought-*

**TABLE 5.4**  Satisfaction-to-Time-Effort Ratios and Classroom
Teacher Behavior

| Satisfaction or Perceived Benefits (material, social, or personal) | Perceived High Time Effort (exhaustion—disability) | Perceived Low Time Effort (fluency—vitality) |
| --- | --- | --- |
| High satisfaction (energizing) | Active participant in reform process, but *at risk for burnout* | Leadership in reform process; *commitment or active participant* |
| Low satisfaction (debilitating) | Dissenter in reform process; *at risk for dropout* | Follower in reform process; at risk for plateauing; *minimum commitment; follower or passive participant* |

*after behavior in the school organization, then educational leaders have to take steps to both increase satisfaction or worth and reduce time effort so that the resulting ratio is higher than that for other competing time-consuming activities in a teacher's life.* Correspondingly, school organizational responses and behaviors of lack of commitment to the welfare of teachers, use of constant evaluation and re-evaluation of teacher effort, encouraging negative politics of the workplace, overloading with paperwork, and/or fostering minimal respect for teachers only result in the lowering of the *S/TE* ratio and thus reduce the attractiveness of teacher participation in these extra time-consuming activities of the school organization.

Using the perspective of the *S/TE* ratio, teachers can exercise appropriate levels of participation to successfully affect needed school reform and change. Teachers can exercise high levels of extra time participation (leadership), they can exercise average but constant levels of extra time participation (active participant), they can also give lip service and provide only minimum levels of extra time participation (minimum participation—a follower) as a plateaued teacher, or they can exercise high levels of time in active opposition to the school reform effort (active dissenter) and provide no time to the effort itself.

## Commitment (Perceived High Compensation–
## Low Time Effort): Tendencies Toward Leadership

The committed classroom teacher in the school organization and the committed school organization work together and judiciously invest time to affect both professional development of the teacher and school change and reform. The elements needed for producing commitment or harmony between teachers and school organizations is high satisfaction or compensation (salary, friend-colleague relationship, social, personal pride, psychological development) associated with the activity and strategies to reduce time effort (fluency in the teaching act, efforts to reduce time inefficiency). For committed teachers, teaching really is worth their time effort.

Following are some descriptions of committed teachers from the perspective of school administrators, fellow teachers, and students being taught by these teachers in the classroom.

An administrator looks at and describes a committed teacher (a teacher who gets satisfaction from teaching and feels that teaching is really worth his or her time):

> The teacher who loves teaching experiences the joy of the teaching career. You can observe a contagious enthusiasm that permeates the classroom. When this teacher teaches, there is no doubt that the students are engaged and learning. Parents will request that their child is assigned to this teacher; the teacher's reputation precedes him or her. This teacher usually doesn't retire on the job, instead he or she teaches as long as possible and is constantly changing professional behaviors to match changing conditions. They are excellent at what they do in the classrooms. They often will take on work after school and participate in extra school activities.

Note the descriptions of perceived high satisfaction and low time effort or fluency.

Compare this description with a teacher-training student's description of a committed teacher:

> A key quality shared by all committed teachers who I have had in my life is flexibility. They all seem to be able to adapt to

virtually any given situation without "skipping a beat." They go with the flow and change, and they always seem to have time for their students to meet different conditions. In classroom discussions, they are able to allow students to express themselves (whether in conflict or agreement with instructor or other students).

Another graduate student added to this description:

The committed teacher understands the far-reaching effects of their efforts in a child's life. They do not take that responsibility lightly. In fact, they are energized by the interaction between teacher and student. They share success without taking any credit away from the student. They overcome failure and take the pressure of it off their students. A committed teacher is always optimistic. They view every child as having a purpose. The respect they earn is not grounded in fear, but rather through care and understanding. They are able to maintain an authoritative position in the classroom through learning and not yelling.

Note again the need for teaching fluency and high satisfaction.

Finally, here are the perspectives of two classroom teachers. The first is from a veteran teacher:

Dedication to themselves, their job, school, students' parents, families, and, of course, their students (all of them) is visible for all to see in a committed teacher. The good students always managed to find their way into their classrooms and offices. Without question, they attract students. Students want them to be their counselor, tutor, adviser, and mostly their friend. They always have time for a student.

Second, here's a younger teacher's view of teaching:

I live for this school; everything else in my life right now is secondary. This is my career. At this point in my life it is what I want to do and I spent most of my time establishing my career.

Note perceived high satisfaction in relation to time effort.

The linkage between satisfaction (compensation) and time effort (fluency) was underscored in this description of this committed teacher from another undergraduate student:

> An important characteristic that comes to mind when thinking of a committed teacher is the actual, noticeable enjoyment that he or she gets from teaching (compensation). The students could always tell that Mr. F had fun teaching his class. He enjoyed the class discussions and hearing students' views on the subject matter. I remember him standing in front of the class with a huge smile on his face whenever a student expressed his differing opinion. . . . He took the time to grade all 120 tests, and did not consider multiple-choice testing to "save time."

In summary, most committed teachers seem to have as a common characteristic the ability to get high satisfaction or compensation or worth from the teaching experience (especially social compensation), and correspondingly they are very good or fluent at what they do and thus have perceived a low time effort.

### Burnout (Perceived High Compensation–High Time Effort): Tendencies Toward Participation

The burned-out teacher is a special type of teacher that came into the profession committed and, even though satisfaction might still be high, time effort is also high, yielding an average to low overall S/TE ratio. The burned-out teacher can be salvaged by school policies to reduce time effort in the school organizations. Because it is somewhat easier to lower time effort than it is to increase satisfaction, leadership in this area should be easier to attain.

Satisfaction can also be increased with certain school leadership policies that involve time, such as release time. The typical satisfaction-boosting pecuniary and nonpecuniary benefits are salary, class size, professional status, and increased fringe benefits. For burned-out teachers, teaching is almost not worth their time effort. The following is a school administrator's perception of a burned-out teacher (a teacher not getting satisfaction from teaching regardless of time effort).

> The burned-out teacher perhaps at one time had the passion for teaching, but as the years progressed, has lost the "fire." They

sadly become negative and at their low point they may even dis-like their peers, students, and parents. They shouldn't be around kids and are sometimes encouraged to change careers or retire from the profession. Social and economic pressures have greatly increased the number of teachers who feel this way to-ward teaching in the school organizations. The lack of effective staff development programs has also made their rehabilitation difficult.

Note the emphasis on perceived lowered satisfaction.

Compare this description with a graduate student's description of a burned-out teacher:

Mrs. S frequently distributed assignments that students were re-quired to work on in class over a period of days. I have no idea what she was doing while her students completed the work, but I know that she was not assisting us. The class watched a great deal of movies, some of which correlated to novels that we were reading. However, the students were never required to discuss the movies in conjunction with the novels. It seemed like she was conveniently "filling time" in the classroom. Mrs. S rarely stood in front of the class and lectured, or held class discussions. She was more of a distant authority figure who assigned activi-ties or papers and then gave us grades. She wasn't into teaching.

Note that because perceived satisfaction is low, the teacher adjusts by lowering the time effort.

The student offered some reasons for the burned-out condition of this teacher in the classroom:

I think there are a few reasons why Mrs. S displayed the charac-teristics of a burned-out teacher. First, I believe that some of the fault can be attributed to the many years that she had spent teaching—I think that she had been teaching for over 25 years. Another reason, I think, had to do with the range of students that she had taught during my senior year. Mrs. S had two classes of AP English students and three classes of regular, jun-ior English classes. Possibly, she felt the AP students were so "ad-vanced" that we could teach ourselves, and so saved her teach-ing efforts for the students that she felt needed more time. I am not trying to make excuses for her teaching methods, but attempting to understand why she cared so little about her students in my class.

Here are a teacher's comments on a burned-out teacher in the school organization:

> The teacher had been at the high school for at least 30 years, and it showed. Unfortunately, he did not share his experience and knowledge with his students in a positive manner. Rather, he appeared aloof, uncaring, even cantankerous. He was an old man, who exuded contempt for the school organization and the "new" generation of students. Clearly, he no longer wanted to be in the classroom or at school, but was waiting for retirement. . . . This teacher had no more passion for his job or position and had little compassion for the students he taught.

Another teacher describes classroom burnout at her school site:

> In the last few years we have had a school site management program, a teacher teaming program, an interdisciplinary teaching program in arts and language, an inclusion of special education student program, and a content mastery program in mathematics. We have had to make so many changes so quickly at our school that no teacher has time to do any of them well. This led to an enormous work overload and the teachers reacted by simply "giving up" and not really participating in any of the programs, and if they did participate, they participated with low levels of commitment.

Finally, another teacher describes her burnout in the classroom as a result of the number of changes she was supposed to accommodate:

> The really sad part of all these school reforms is that there are so many changes going on at the same time that the outstanding classroom teachers, who really want to teach children, are diverted to service these changes. They eventually burn out of the teaching profession and because of little value to the change effort.

The large amount of hours, outside of school time, that is needed for these reforms is simply too much for the average teacher with a family. It is not that the reform itself has no educational merit, but there is so little time given to properly implement the reform that it is done badly, hence all of our time and effort is wasted.

Note that most of the emphasis in these descriptions is on the need for increased satisfaction and lower time effort.

Sometimes poor working conditions at a school site directly affect the quality of the teacher's life. Student transiency at a school site can become a significant factor in lowering satisfaction and raising the time effort of the classroom teacher. Here is one teacher's view of classroom time effort at a school with large numbers of transient students:

In general, I have to review rules and routines, teacher classroom procedures, and take needed time away from instruction to make these new children feel welcome in the classroom. In most instances, these new students require more before- and after-school individual help with classwork and homework. All of the clerical activities associated with intra-year transiency added to my workload and take away valuable time from the instructional program and other students in my class.

Note the increasing perceived time effort and the lowering of satisfaction as a result of time effort increases.

But by far, school organizations themselves became the major source of teacher burnout—even if the intentions of the administration are well meaning. Here is one teacher's comment regarding how a math school reform project increased her time effort and lowered her satisfaction at school:

I missed 12 days of instruction while I became part of a math reform project. My students lost 12 days of instruction at the expense of this educational reform. Maybe 2% of the population of students would have benefited from the math reform. It was difficult for a teacher to come in and sub for me and for me to pick up where she left off. In essence, I had to do double duty and it became overwhelming, and I wound up not enjoying either activity.

Note how the increasing time effort resulted in lowering satisfaction.

Many of these burned-out teachers had a common characteristic: high time effort. That high time effort was associated with a lowering of perceived satisfaction of teaching in the school organization. Because the age of a teacher naturally increases time effort due to possible physiological changes that might occur with age, the $S/TE$ ratio is an important concept for education leaders to appreciate. If, for example, satisfaction does not increase correspondingly as time effort increases, then the $S/TE$ becomes lower and the teacher will eventually burn out of the profession. If time effort gets extremely high and satisfaction lowers, then these same teachers will want to drop out of the profession, seek early retirement, or "psychologically retire" while still being classroom teachers. If teachers have to stay in the profession solely because it is the only way for them to earn a living, then their unhappiness over time-consuming school reforms and changes will reflect in their teaching. Unhappy teachers with low $S/TE$ ratios ultimately affect the quality of student learning in the classroom. It is important to stress that although actual clock time might be low, it is the perceived effort behind the time that is most troublesome for effective leadership.

### Dropout (Perceived Low Compensation–High Time Effort): Tendencies Toward Opposition and Dissension

Potential drop-out teachers or minimal commitment teachers are a particularly difficult problem for educational leaders because they have both low satisfaction and high perceived time effort. These drop-out teachers really want to be in some other profession and be working outside of the classroom. For a variety of reasons, however, some teachers stay in the teaching profession and essentially "do time" in the classroom as they wait for retirement. Typically, these teachers become centers of negativity and active dissent in the school organization. One of the major impediments to school reform and change efforts is teachers who are dissatisfied with teaching itself. For drop-out teachers, teaching is perceived as not being worth their time effort, but they teach anyway.

One school administrator describes a drop-out teacher:

The drop-out teacher realizes early on this is not the career they feel comfortable with. Discipline, control, and organization are not their strong points, and they lack the self-confidence to do the job. Not everyone can or should teach, and they may be able to utilize some of their teacher training in another profession. Unfortunately, many of these teachers hang on since teaching is the only well-paying job they feel they can do.

Compare the above description with a graduate student's description of a drop-out teacher:

I had a teacher who really did not like his students. This teacher had a side business and would come to school merely for the retirement benefits and would do just enough to get by. All we did was work on problems he would place on the board and he rarely lectured. He only gave time-efficient true-false tests. Being in his class was a waste of our time as well as his time.

A fellow teacher comments on the drop-out teacher:

We have many teachers at our school who do the absolute minimum to get by. They have tenure, they get raises like the rest of us and just show up and leave. They are not interested in either the kids, the school, or their fellow teachers. We don't even get together socially. Unfortunately, I am seeing more and more teachers who exhibit this type of behavior at school.

Finally, another teacher points to low satisfaction and high time effort as a source of her potentially giving up on the profession:

When I go to school, I really have more than one full-time job. I have to supervise 150 kids without any support and instructional materials. Teachers have to do more activities in the classroom and have to do it with less time, no support from the school, and no funds to see that it is done well and evaluated for effectiveness. Sometimes, I wonder what I am doing here, and when I look at other professionals in the workforce and what they have as part of their jobs, I get a little envious.

Although very few in number, the drop-out teacher has enormous impact on school culture and student learning. The drop-out classroom teacher is at the last stage of declining satisfaction and increasing time effort. They derive nearly zero material, social, or psychological compensation from classroom teaching. Many of these teachers begin the process of switching their energies and time efforts to activities that are located outside of the school organization. Protected by tenure, these teachers during a 35-year career in the classroom can do enormous damage to the learning process of children and the evolution of the school organization. Finally, these drop-out teachers also project a poor teaching image of the self to students and to the public. Drop-out teachers, unlike burned-out teachers, have reached the terminal stage of their professional development and are unsalvageable with regard to participation in school reform and change. Attempts by school leaders for school reform and change, therefore, basically have to be engineered around their opposition. Better teacher preparation and selection, better inservice training, and better mentoring and counseling are almost the only ways to deal with the problem and ensure that these teachers, who wish to do time in the classroom, never enter the teaching profession. This should be the objective of preservice training. Time-sensitive leadership has to ensure that no classroom teacher evolves to this state in the school organization.

### *Pushout (Perceived Low Compensation–Low Time Effort): Tendencies Toward Marginal Commitment*

Pushed-out or marginalized teachers would like to contribute more to the school organization in terms of participation in change and reform activities, but can't find the needed time in their busy lives to engage in the process. In some instances, the politics of the workplace results in their not being invited to participate, even though they might have a great deal to contribute. Even though they become professionally productive in the classroom, they are plateaued in the school organization. The pushed-out teacher is of particular importance to the school organization because these teachers have much to contribute to school reform debate in terms of professional memory of what works and what does not. Pushing out plateaued, good teachers can be viewed as a form of passive aggressive behavior on the part of the school organization. This type of classroom teacher practice of pushing out teachers by excessive time demands or politics of the workplace is very unprofessional, tends to destroy organizational loyalty, and lowers morale for all class-room teachers. Pushout and politics also create an incentive for the talented, but pushed-out, teacher to sell time to other organizations that are more appreciative of their time investment. The school or-ganization with large numbers of pushed-out teachers usually expe-riences rapid and widespread turnover among its professional staff. If staff turnover is high, the spirit of the school organization suffers. For pushed-out teachers, teaching could be worth their time effort, but they perceive little support and encouragement for their efforts.

The transference of time from classroom responsibilities to fam-ily responsibilities is extremely common among classroom teachers. The following is a typical example of the "time transfer" by a class-room teacher who likes the teaching profession, but can't provide the time needed by the school organization or is not invited to par-ticipate in the reform and change process:

> I always need more time in the morning so that I can leave my kid off at the baby-sitters. In the afternoon, I leave school early so that I can pick her up. I used to spend time after school work-ing on lesson plans; now I really need this time for myself and my family. There is simply no time to do both family and school, and my family comes first.

Note the comments by this pushed-out teacher on the school or-ganization:

> Now the school wants me to actually help them run the school that I teach at. I went into teaching to teach children, not to be a manager of adults. If I wanted to be a manager, I would have gotten an MBA in college instead of a teaching credential. I don't want to do things in my life that I don't care about, or I don't want to be a part of an activity that I am not given the opportu-nity to do well. I want my time focused in learning and instruc-tion.

A similar theme is reflected in the comments of this pushed-out teacher:

The school administrators tell us that this reform is new. But I am an older teacher, so I've seen it before only in a different form. My philosophy in dealing with school reforms is that this too shall pass. The school seems to enjoy setting teachers up for failing and then when the reform doesn't work the teacher is blamed as being an impediment to change. The school administration should be asking why the reform is needed in the first place—how sure are they that it works in a real-world classroom setting? I ignore all these reforms and imagine that it is a "welfare project" for politicians and administrators to justify their position. Rather than developing a reform to genuinely help the classroom teacher, the reforms never get to the point that it really helps kids learn.

Another teacher stated,

There is no way I will go through all these reforms at my school. It used to be that teachers had the time to take care of their life needs outside of the school environment as well as in the classroom. Lately, all this time has been taken away. I won't have my family take a back seat to my job as a teacher.

From another age-related pushed-out teacher:

My young teaching colleague is very modern and doesn't use a book in her classroom. I have observed her and the older teachers like myself with regard to our teaching. My experience is that using the book is best. I am not going to change what works best for me in the classroom. Younger teachers can do what they want to do, but they don't have the experience of knowing what works and what doesn't work. I think they are more gullible, and I don't want their views imposed on me in terms of how I teach.

Finally, some teachers challenge the worth of some of the extra time expenditures that are needed for school reform:

I don't want to use my time to team teach in the classroom when there are other things I would rather do with my time in the classroom. Teaming in teaching is just too much work for me, and I don't think it benefits students.

## Summary

Classroom teachers are strongly motivated by the need for time investment balance in their time-consuming activities. First, there are time-consuming activities that take the general form of material compensation in a society where earning a living is a major challenge. Second, there are time-consuming activities that are associated with having a life outside of the school organization. These activities include developing social relationships with families, friends, and students. Finally, there are time-consuming activities associated with personal or psychological development. These are time investments needed for the self and include time for hobbies, recreation, and interests.

> When a time-consuming school activity infringes on time needed for other time-consuming activities in a teacher's life, professional and psychological conflict occurs.

When a time-consuming activity of a school infringes on time needed for other time-consuming activities in a teacher's life, professional and psychological conflict occurs. Because time investment for a classroom teacher is paced by a linear clock and deducted from a finite amount of time in a lifetime, time for one time-consuming activity in life is taken at the expense of another time-consuming activity. The balance of time demands, as reflected in the organizational versus teacher time investments, is really an armistice between the teacher's material existence and lifestyle satisfaction, on one hand, and the school organization's quest for legitimacy and visibility, on the other hand. Ideally, after-school or extra time-consuming activities have to be designed so that time needs are met for both the individual teacher's needs with regard to lifestyle satisfaction and the school organization's needs with regard to increased legitimacy and visibility in society. Time is, therefore, a currency of exchange used to purchase both objectives. For more mature teachers, or midcareer teachers who will not see the return on their added school organizational time investments, time considerations and conflicts are particularly important and can become a major impediment to school reform and change. Finally, time exchanges between the classroom teacher and the school organization can lead to observed teacher behaviors of commitment, burnout, pushout, and dropout.

## Perspectives, Points of View, Discussion

- How can teacher compensation schemes be changed to create incentives for placing all teachers on a similar professional development clock so that they can participate in the reform and change process?
- What are different kinds of incentives that can be offered to older teachers? to younger teachers?
- What effect do unhappy and resentful teachers participating in school reform activities have on the overall objectives of the school reform movement?
- In your experience, have you noticed any differences between school reforms as designed by school leaders and school reforms as delivered by classroom teachers?
- Do you think that commitment, pushout, burnout, and dropout are time related?
- Have you ever encountered teachers who have been pushed out of the reform process and school organizational participation because of excessive time demands?
- Are older teachers really that different from younger teachers with regard to time perceptions, time investments, and time sensitivity?
- Do you think that time control will become a major collective bargaining issue by unions in the near or distant future?

## NOTE

1. This quote and other quotes in this chapter, unless otherwise noted, are from personal interviews with teachers and graduate students.

# 6

# Putting Your School in Prime Time: Getting Commitment

*I despise making the most of one's time. Half the pleasures of life consists of the opportunities one has neglected.*

OLIVER WENDELL HOLMES

- Educational Leadership in an Era of Time Scarcity
- Management of the Change and Reform Process
- Developing Strategies for Increasing Teacher Time Commitment to School Change and Reform
- Some Radical Strategies to Encourage Teacher Participation in Reform
- Summary
- Perspectives, Points of View, Discussion

## Educational Leadership in an Era of Time Scarcity

Putting your school organization in prime time implies that harmony in time between the classroom teaching staff and the educational leaders of the school organization has been reached. Prime time means that teachers are finding lifestyle satisfaction from their time investments, and school organizations are enhancing their legitimacy and positive visibility in the community for their time investments. For many classroom teachers, lifestyle satisfaction can be related to time investments to attain money, power, position, recognition, control, and professional development. For school organizations, change and reform time investments are rewarded with more influence, greater funding, more enhanced legitimacy, and positive visibility in the community. Change and reform time investments for both teachers and school organizations should not be viewed as a loss of the old ways of doing things, but instead should be considered as a win-win opportunity for professional growth for the classroom teacher and productivity for the school organization.

> Educational leadership in an era of time scarcity is particularly difficult in school organizations because it is based on the reconciliation of the two types of clocks to pace time passage (linear and cyclical) and the two types of goals and objectives (lifestyle satisfaction and societal legitimacy).

The notion of authority, hierarchy, obligation, and tradition, common to past generations of teachers, has rapidly given way to non-tradition-bound teaching behaviors in the classroom. In the past, teachers used to look to mature teachers, school leaders, and school principals as role models of professional behavior in the classroom. The future vision for themselves as professional educators was thus intergenerationally transmitted. Now many teachers look to more unrealistic TV models of teaching behavior (to be cool), define for themselves what their teaching role should be, or else identify only with certain groups of teachers (young, old, black, white, elementary, secondary, male, female) with regard to their teaching behavior in the classroom. Becoming a master teacher in the traditional sense, over a long career in the classroom, is not worth attaining for many younger teachers. For those with low interest in the past (memory) and little interest in attaining a future vision for themselves as professional educators, present behavior shows a desire to just get by in the classroom with minimal time effort.

When the psychological bonds between teaching generations and between school administrators and classroom teachers are broken, gone is any notion of tradition and loyalty to the school organization. Unfortunately, school reform is a voluntary time-consuming activity for a classroom teacher. Because it is voluntary, school reform is tied to a teacher's vision for the future.

---

The key to voluntary participation is to make the activity worth the time effort of the teacher and to have a high satisfaction to time effort ratio.

---

One really can't force teachers to do anything on their own time unless they are committed to the activity and have a vision for its use in their lives—psychologically or professionally. If forced to participate while being noncommitted, teachers will act with passive-aggressive behaviors, and their resentment toward the school organization will increase. The key to voluntary participation is to make the activity worth the time effort of the teacher and to have a high satisfaction to time effort (*S/TE*) ratio.

Previous chapters examined the important role that time, as a currency of exchange, plays in understanding the behaviors of classroom teachers in school organizations. The linear time frame perspective in the life of a teacher and the cyclical time frame perspective in the evolution of school organizations were given particular attention. It is the differences in time frame perspectives that are the genesis of many of the observed time conflicts between classroom teachers and school organizations. This chapter examines some of the specific time-sensitive issues of classroom teachers that are associated with school reform and change. This chapter also provides strategies for educational leaders to use in addressing time investment conflicts in an era of time scarcity.

These are some of the time-leadership issues that will be presented in this chapter.

• Time constraints or time scarcity in a teacher's lifetime will tend to worsen in the coming decades because of increased time pressure and personal demands associated with material, social, and personal

development compensation. To service the time needs of anticipated school reforms, getting extra time from classroom teachers
will be much more difficult. Time control will also become a hotly
contested issue in collective bargaining negotiations between
teacher unions and classroom teachers.

• The demographic trend of single-parent homes will continue,
and a teaching position being the sole source of income will create
added incentives for teachers to moonlight—or sell any available
free time—or give more of their time to their families and not provide time on a voluntary basis to the school organization.

• Redesigns of instructional delivery—using modern technologies—will have a great impact on a teacher's sense of personal time
control in the classroom. With technology, single-teacher teaching
might be replaced by team teaching. These changes in educational
delivery will affect the role of a classroom teacher in student learning and will attract different types of individuals to the teaching profession. In essence, individual teacher time control might be replaced by group or team time control, lessening, for some teachers, a
major nonpecuniary benefit.

• Developing teacher loyalty to the school organization should be a
top priority for educational leaders. Loyalty of teachers is essentially
built on memory of classroom teaching over long periods of time.
Teacher memory also becomes an important part of engineering successful school reforms and change in the school organization. Memory of past teaching practices that failed or were successful in actual
classroom settings can affect behavior exhibited in present teaching
practices, which, in turn, can affect a teacher's future vision of teaching. *Eliminating or devaluing the memory of older teachers, and correspondingly overvaluing the views of younger teachers, not only
devalues loyalty and expertise, it places educational leaders in the precarious position of designing school reforms that might not be effective in the classroom.*

• To increase teacher participation rates and investments in the
multitude of extra-time school-related activities, educational leaders
will have to design participation strategies that increase satisfaction
or worth or perceived benefits to teachers and decrease their time

effort. The $S/TE$ ratio thus becomes an important element for voluntary participation in the extra time-consuming activities of the school organization.

• The numerous waves of school reforms in public education, all requiring—but not explicitly considering—the need for more of a teacher's time effort, and a corresponding lowering of teacher satisfaction, have created a situation where any attempt at future school reforms will be discredited or compared to those reforms that failed in the past. The demonstration that school learning is actually improved with a reform is a burden-of-proof responsibility that has to be assumed by educational leaders.

• The management of the change and reform process in school organizations, based on the perspective of time, has to be directed at resolving some of the linear time frame demands of classroom teachers (life and lifestyle satisfaction) and the cyclical time frame demands of the school organization (evolution and productivity).

The ultimate goal of building teacher commitment to the school organization in an era of time scarcity is thus based on the construct of "time investment" and the ratio of $S/TE$ for the time-consuming activity. To increase teacher participation rates and time investment in school reform efforts, the school organization will have to align itself, in time, to the world of the classroom teacher (see Table 6.1).

In the research literature, leadership in work organizations has been approached from a general viewpoint of organizational demands on the individual with the research of Colarusso (1994), Hassard (1991), Howard and Bray (1988), and Lomranz, Friedman, Gitter, Shmotkin, and Medini (1985); and commitment with the research of Becker (1960).

School issues that are associated with leadership and time investment can be found in the research of Ben-Peretz and Bromme (1990) and Cutler and Ruopp (1993). The career paths of teachers (Milstein, 1990a, 1990b), especially plateauing, have also been explored in the educational research literature.

Finally, the specific role that time plays in school reform can be found in the research of Fullan and Miles (1992), Hannaway and Carnoy (1993), and Johansen (1992). Suggestions for school reform and change can be found in Purnell and Hill (1992), and time needed

**TABLE 6.1** Time-Harmony Considerations for Increasing Teacher
Participation Rates in the School Reform and Change
Process

| *Teacher Concerns* | *Organizational Concerns* |
|---|---|
| Lower personal time effort | Lower resource |
| Needs to make the reform viable in the classroom | Needs to make the reform economically viable |
| ↓ | ↓ |
| Increase perceived professional or psychological benefits to students in the classroom | Increase perceived school output benefits to students |
| ↓ | ↓ |
| Acknowledge constraints of a linear time frame | Acknowledge constraints of a cyclical time frame |

by classroom teachers for collaboration in Raywid (1993). One study
(Sarason, 1990) suggests that most school reforms are predictable in
terms of failure to be implemented largely because of time.

The important challenge for educational leadership is, therefore, to provide the time for reform to be more time sensitive. "Creating time for reform requires time investments. Teachers have to invest extra time and energy as participants in restructuring schools.
The needs for time and resource are interlocking" (Purnell & Hill,
1992, p. 11).

This theme is continued when the authors refer to time policies
of the school organization: "Time is an important resource for
changing schools. The challenge to those who direct or influence
public education is to adopt policies and programs that take into
consideration the role that time assumes in bringing about change in
the schools" (Purnell & Hill, 1992, p. 37).

Finding time, therefore, is a major impediment to school reform
efforts because it requires substituted committee and collaborative
time from classroom teachers (Watkins, 1993; Watts & Castle, 1993;
West, 1990). Collaboration and committee time requires that many
teachers be in sync with regard to time. Note the time implications associated with the various types of school reforms. It would be interesting

**TABLE 6.2** Emphases of School Reform

| | |
|---|---|
| Instructional reform | Emphasis on a specific tool or educational practice |
| Structural reform | Emphasis on governance and the structure of the school organization |
| Curriculum reform | Emphasis on what is taught to children |
| Pedagogical reform | Emphasis on how curriculum and specific subject matter are taught |
| Assessment and evaluation reform | Emphasis on methods for assessing what is taught |

to examine these reforms from the perspective of the classroom teacher, especially with regard to the *S/TE* ratio (see Table 6.2).

Classroom teachers have expressed their feelings toward some reforms by active dissension, ignoring the reform, modifying the reform, or in rare instances, embracing the reform. What seems to be an important component of this behavior is the *S/TE* ratio for the teacher. Note that some of the school reform proposals, as designed by educational leaders, would actually increase time effort and lower satisfaction for teachers. The net result of not engineering the concept of time into any school reform effort sets the reform up for failure when it reaches the implementation phase in the classroom.

A few school reforms and their hypothesized implications for the *S/TE* ratio for classroom teachers are shown in Table 6.3. Educational leaders should realize that if the *S/TE* ratio is high enough, classroom teachers will find the time or substitute one time-consuming activity for another time-consuming activity to ensure its success in the classroom. The fact that nearly every school reform effort over the past decade has referred to "time" as the most limiting resource supports the need to closely examine the *S/TE* ratio associated with the reform effort.

Additionally, school reforms that depend on teacher time spent on bookkeeping, paperwork, and managing school operations instead of direct student contact is not what most teachers had in mind when they decided to enter the teaching profession. School reforms that require large amounts of teacher time effort will also not be well

**TABLE 6.3** Effects of Various Reforms on Satisfaction to Time Effort Ratio

| Reform Activity | Hypothesized Impact on the S/TE Ratio |
|---|---|
| Detracking | Lower S, higher TE |
| Year-round schooling | Higher S, lower TE (for some teachers the reverse is true) |
| Charter schools | Higher S, higher TE |
| Site-based management | Higher S, higher TE |
| Technology | Higher S, lower TE |
| Curriculum reform | Higher S, higher TE |
| Teacher certification | Higher S, higher TE |
| Assessment reform | Lower S, higher TE |

NOTE: S = satisfaction; TE = time effort.

received because even if satisfaction remains constant, time effort increases, hence lowering the S/TE ratio.

Sometimes reforms are generated by teachers themselves, and school administrative personnel conclude that "it is not important enough" for the school organization. As one teacher noted:[1]

> A few years ago we teachers agreed to work in teams to help kids in the classroom. After all the time and effort we put into the program, the school administration pulled the plug because it was too much trouble to schedule students with teachers.

Unfortunately, some classroom teachers view recent school reforms efforts as being unattractive from a teaching perspective or as a complete waste of their time. To ask teachers for additional time investment from their lifetimes for poorly thought-out school reforms is futile, especially when there are other time-consuming activities in a teacher's life and there is no threat to job security. A school reform effort that is not worth the teacher's time will not only cause a great amount of stress in a teacher's life but, if implemented anyway, will usually fail when delivered to the classroom setting by the teacher.

Consider, for example, recent school reform proposals, such as the Goals 2000 school reform proposed by the federal government. The Goals 2000 reform is not only costly in terms of financial investment, but it will require huge amounts of additional time investment on the part of classroom teachers. Some of the teacher time implications for the school reforms specified in the Goals 2000 project include the following:

1. *Children will start school ready to learn.* How much teacher time and effort will be required to teach children who have impoverished backgrounds to be ready for school?
2. *High school graduation rates will increase to 90%.* How many teachers will have to stay after school and take the time out of their lifetimes to ensure that these students are ready for graduation?
3. *U.S. students will be competent in a core of academic subjects.* What teaching faculty will provide the needed time to their teaching load to ensure that all students reach the competency levels needed?
4. *U.S. students will be first in the world in mathematics.* This is perhaps the most unrealistic time-intensive goal of all, because mathematics is a time-sequenced subject. How much time and what curriculum and teacher delivery systems will have to be in place to guarantee meeting this goal?

The Goals 2000 school reform activity is currently financed with $393 million in federal funds. The actual cost for this reform, however, will be paid in millions of extra hours of teacher time. It will be time that will be largely uncompensated and drawn from the lifetimes of the teachers. Economic viability, financial feasibility, and political acceptability are criteria for the evaluation of Goals 2000 that would have to be met if the reform as designed by the government is actually delivered to the classroom. If, on the other hand, teachers are fully compensated for their added time effort (thereby increasing $S$) and if technology is employed to lower the time effort required (thereby lowering $TE$), then the higher resulting $S/TE$ ratio will ensure that this type of school reform might be feasible both in design and in actual delivery to the classroom.

Because many of the proposed school reforms have a heavy component in the area of technology, it is important to explicitly consider how these technologies can affect teacher time. In general, technology-based school reforms are initially well received because they are designed to lower teacher time effort in the classroom. There is an important caveat, however. The introduction of massive amounts of sophisticated computer and multimedia technology also requires enormous amounts of teacher training time and initial preparation of materials. The technology first has to be learned and then adapted by the classroom teacher for it to be fully effective and truly integrated into classroom instruction. Unfortunately, the technology itself quickly becomes outdated. A revolving door of teacher training, therefore, is set in motion with the need to relearn these technologies before the benefits of the older technology are realized in the classroom. The time needed to learn the new technology as well as the time needed to keep up with the subject matter are both drawn from the same finite amount of time in the lifetime of the teacher. *The inability of teachers to recover these large amounts of invested time over their careers in the classroom makes the school reform effort slow to implement and difficult to maintain.*

Subject matter specialists such as science and mathematics teachers, of course, might be far more sympathetic and responsive to certain types of technological reforms and change in the schools. The reason for this acceptance is that these classroom teachers already have a significant time investment advantage because their field is already involved with technology. These teachers are already predisposed to learn new developments in technology to stay current. Their satisfaction level would thus increase because of their subject matter expertise. In essence, they would see the direct relevance of the newer technologies to their classroom teaching interests (increasing $S$), they are fluent in learning the newer technologies (lowering $TE$), and they have to learn the technologies anyway (polychronometric).

The elementary school specialist, on the other hand, might be more oriented toward a traditional student-teacher interactive role of teaching and would thus perceive the time needed to learn the new technologies as an added time requirement that takes away from direct student contact.

## Management of the Change and Reform Process

"If teachers could only 'see the light' on the need for and the effectiveness of school reforms, then these reforms would be in every state of the union and educational achievement would soar." This is the typical position of many school reformers and educational leaders when trying to convince teachers to provide the extra time to participate in school reform efforts. *The fact that resistance by teachers to school reform and change efforts is so pervasive and powerful should lead one to suspect that the important resource of time and time investment is being ignored.* Possibly, the problem lies in the way teachers are compensated.

The U.S. public school model of compensation evolved primarily from a "scientific management" view of teacher effort in the classroom. It was a view of compensation based on two dimensions (experience and highest academic degree). With this type of compensation system, classroom teachers were considered to be workers who merely had to account for their contract time. Administrators, on the other hand, were school leaders who managed that contract time. Compensation with this type of model required conformity by teachers in a hierarchical school work organization where time commitments were precisely defined. Teacher compensation schemes were then placed in standardized steps based only on experience (time) and education or academic units completed. Control over teacher time in the classroom with the fixed-step salary model went from top administration down to the classroom teacher level. There was little involvement by teachers in outside-of-school classroom activities because there was no compensation provided and it wasn't part of the teaching contract. A professional corps of school administrators or educational leaders with higher salaries and an 11-month school year contract emerged as a professional class to actively invest their time from their lifetimes to manage the schools and thus provide any needed extra time. In short, teachers were expected to teach, and administrators were expected to manage. There was a functional division of labor where teachers taught children with their time investments, and administrators managed fiscal resources and planned for change in the organization with their time investments.

As the teaching profession changes, different forms of compensation and salary schedules will be required.

In the late 1980s and early 1990s, schools changed in governance and became more characterized by teacher workforce diversity and a significant involvement of teachers in both the management of the school organization and instruction in the classroom. With reform, schools became far more decentralized regarding school site management and school site decision making. Today, we have far more teacher-parent-administration time involvement and participation in the school organization. Shared decision making for instruction and management implies not only larger amounts of formal classroom time from teachers to provide instruction but also huge amounts of extra teacher time for the management of activities outside of the classroom. As the teaching profession changes with regard to expected time investments and teachers no longer are isolated in their classrooms, different forms of compensation and salary schedules will be required. Professional development of teachers will be a lifelong process, and the scope of this development will have to include time for training, not only in subject matter areas and pedagogy but also in school site change and management skills. Whereas time under the former model was precisely compensated in terms of salary by years of service and longevity in the organization, future models of compensation will have to include compensation for extra time investments by classroom teachers in the school organization.

The redefinition of the role of the classroom teacher to encompass management skills will obviously require more teacher preparation time investment, more service time investment, and more professional development time investment over the career of the classroom teacher. Graduate students who are far more disposed to this new type of teacher will thus enter teacher training programs at our colleges and universities. Finally, children in the classroom will also become far more difficult to teach as a result of social problems such as drug abuse, divorce, poverty, limited English fluency, and so forth. The great distinctions between various types of school organizations in the future might not be on race (black schools–white schools) or economic status (rich schools–poor schools) but on the marginal cost or degree of difficulty of teaching (easy to teach-difficult to teach) at certain school sites. School sites might be classified as schools where children are relatively easy to teach with large amounts of home support requiring relatively low time effort in the classroom (charter and magnet schools) and schools where children will be very difficult to teach with low satisfaction requiring high time effort on the part of classroom teachers.

In short, if satisfaction or compensation of classroom teachers does not increase to meet the higher time effort demands in the classroom, then public schools will be characterized by huge numbers of burned-out, pushed-out, and dropped-out teachers. No school reform or change effort will be successful if it has to be delivered in the classroom by these time-stressed classroom teachers.

## Developing Strategies for Increasing Teacher Time Commitment to School Change and Reform

Following are 25 time-sensitive recommendations and strategies for increasing satisfaction and lowering time effort for classroom teachers engaged in school reform and change efforts.

1. Recognize that time, not money, for most classroom teachers is a crucial lifestyle resource. Give greater attention to organizing school reform activities with regard to time efficiency over cost efficiency. The largest part of the bill for school reform is paid for by the teacher in terms of time taken from their lifetime, not money provided by the taxpayer. The older the teacher in the school organization, the higher subjective perceived value attributed to units of time. The road from teacher capability to teacher competency to teacher proficiency to teacher mastery also requires time. The subjective weighted hour of the classroom teacher, therefore, should be an important concern for educational leaders.

2. Recognize that because of teachers' linear versus school organizations' cyclical time frames, goals and objectives of time investments are usually not congruent. If organizational goals are diffuse and ambiguous, then teachers are less likely to commit their time to the organization, and their $S/TE$ ratio is low. The burden of proof of

time worth for classroom teachers is with the school organization. Presenting scientific proof and convincing arguments that specific school reform activities actually work in the classroom to help a teacher increase satisfaction or reduce time effort would be of enormous help in the management of the change process. Many teachers are marginalized or pushed out of the reform and change process precisely because they remain unconvinced of the efficacy of these reform efforts in actually helping them in the classroom.

3. Those teachers who are marginalized or pushed out (want to change but can't find the time), or have high satisfaction but simply cannot give the needed time, have to somehow be included in the school reform process. One cannot dismiss or devalue their classroom expertise and thus indirectly overvalue the expertise of those teachers who have the time. More important, not including the memory of the older teacher can lead the reform movement down an ineffectual path to reform, that is, make the same mistakes as in the past. In fact, many of those pushed-out teachers might be the best teachers in the school district, and those teachers who have the time to participate might be the marginal teachers.

4. Secondary teachers and subject matter specialists, in particular, would be very difficult to involve in school reform efforts because of the extensive amount of time investments they have to make to their subject matter area to stay current with their field. Some of the best analytical minds to direct school reform efforts and policies (they see the end product) are thus eliminated or pushed out of the school reform and change process. A balance between elementary and secondary classroom teacher participation in school reform and change activities should be sought.

5. Numerous school meetings and after-school meetings that are too long in duration tend to guarantee burnout, dropout, and pushout of teachers, because they lower the $S/TE$ ratio. Fewer, shorter, more time-efficient meetings should be sought to engage more educational personnel in the school reform activity. The lower the time effort, the higher the $S/TE$ ratio and the greater the probability of commitment by teachers to the school reform and change process.

6. Time compression and time efficiency technologies such as videotapes, e-mail, and the Internet should be sought to lower time effort associated with reform and change efforts. If organized properly, time compression technologies can be of important use in school reform and can attract many more of the pushed-out teachers by lowering their time effort.

7. Information-seeking behaviors, associated with school reform efforts, are strongly related to the time investment portfolio of the classroom teacher. If school reform activities require the seeking of information, they must be aligned to compensation objectives of the time investment portfolios of teachers (development of economic capital, social relationship capital, and personal development capital), not only to the objectives of the school organization. The pairing of older with younger teachers to reduce time effort, especially in the area of learning newer computer technologies, is one strategy that can be used to increase participation rates of classroom teachers.

8. The traditional practice of substituting school reform time-consuming activities for class time-consuming activities or paying substitutes to take the teacher's place in the classroom is largely ineffectual in promoting teacher participation. If the teacher has to make up for lost time when the class is taught by a substitute teacher, then nothing is really gained for the regular classroom teacher. In fact, in many instances this practice tends to place additional workloads on the classroom teacher and thus increase their time effort. Careful attention, therefore, should be given to the economic opportunity cost for any released time that is provided by the school organization for classroom teachers to engage in school reform activities.

9. Trading off time from regular class instruction for an extra prep period of time might be an excellent option for most teachers to increase their participation in school reform. This option is especially appropriate for teachers who feel that any time off from regular instructional duties has to be made up later in the classroom. Meetings should only be given when there is something of value or worth to the teacher. At a school organizational meeting, time seems

to pass much more quickly when there is something in it for the teacher or if the teacher feels that the perceived compensation is high. Correspondingly, school meetings seem to drag on when teachers do not see any potential compensation benefit or worth for their time investment. The guiding principle should be: Is the school reform meeting worth the teachers' time?

10. Additional options for enhancing classroom teacher participation rates in school reform efforts might include limiting the number of years a teacher should be allowed to teach a certain class. The "ownership" of a class limitation would stimulate teachers to reinvest time in other courses of the curriculum every 5 years or so and thus naturally promote some of the change and reform goals of the school organization. If teachers feel that they own a class, they are less likely to want to reform and change the curriculum for the course because the current $S/TE$ ratio is high.

11. Unfortunately, many school reforms efforts are directly aimed at reallocating instructional time during the school day or class schedule reform. This type of school reform might set up a situation where the extra time allotted by teachers is actually wasted as teachers have students do homework, have independent study, or have a pseudo study hall so that teacher time effort can be lowered. With school calendar reform, emphasis on curriculum reform to make use of the increased time should be stressed.

12. Paying teachers in school organizations in accordance with how much time they actually invest in school activities, and not merely counting years of service in the district or highest academic degree or college credits beyond the B.A., might be part of the incentive and compensation scheme for attaining the goals of school reform. Teachers generally tend to be comparatively underpaid at the beginning of their careers, when they use their time to establish tenure in the school organization, and are then comparatively overpaid for their services toward the end of their careers, when they use their time in activities outside of the school organization.

13. Recommendations for preservice teacher training programs might include making sure that time orientations and discussions

are made an explicit part of the curricula of teacher training. The long haul of a career in the teaching profession requires that the beginning teacher realizes the unique nature of the school organization-individual teacher time linkage.

14. The devaluation of tradition and teaching expertise is the direct consequence of pushing out the older teacher with memory from the school reform and change process. The devaluation of tradition and expertise can only harm the long-term objectives of the teaching profession because it tends to promote a free agent type of employment mentality among classroom teachers and, eventually, lowers school organization loyalty and morale. Special efforts to attract experienced teachers to the reform effort must be made.

15. Be sure to include time needs of classroom teachers as a budget component when submitting school reform grants. This action will at least permit the school organization to place a dollar value on teacher time in the school reform budget and not consider teacher time as a free resource to be given to the school organization.

16. As much as possible, attempt to be polychronometric with regard to school reform time-consuming activities. The greater the ability to serve two objectives (personal and organizational) with the same hour or unit of time, the higher the satisfaction for the same time effort.

17. Pride of ownership in the school reform activity tends to increase the participation rates of teachers. If classroom teachers feel part of both the initiation of the reform and its implementation, it is more likely that the reform as designed will be the same as the reform as delivered to the classroom. Pride of ownership increases satisfaction and, even if time effort is higher, the $S/TE$ ratio remains high.

18. Teachers tend to rate inservice workshops higher than school reform meetings because they associate the inservice meeting with units of credit toward some form of direct compensation. The $S/TE$ ratio is much higher for inservice meetings because the meetings tend to directly relate to ways of lessening time effort or increasing satisfaction for the teacher in the classroom.

19. In a choice between curricular and pedagogical reforms, older teachers tend to feel that both are not worth their time, whereas younger teachers tend to feel that they both are worth their time. This general tendency might be a result of the impact of the subjective weighted hour for teachers at different ages and stages of their career. In designing school reforms, therefore, important consideration has to be given to subjective time weight of an hour for the classroom teacher. In addition, the expected benefits payoff period in the classroom as a result has to be much shorter for the older teacher.

20. The idea of the classroom teacher "banking" or accumulating time so that this time could be used for planning and reform has been proposed for school organizations. Unfortunately, this strategy tends to lessen instructional time in the classroom and does little to increase the *S/TE* ratio of the teacher.

21. Resolve time conflicts that are directed toward functional outcomes of a school organization and time conflicts that are dysfunctional or not geared toward any legitimate output of the school organization. In addition, be sure that problem areas are precisely defined beforehand so that little time is wasted on activities that have little relationship to the needed reform.

22. One of the most important strategies that schools can employ to enhance teacher time investment is to build strong and effective channels of communication. Classroom teachers and leaders of reform efforts in the school organization have to work in time harmony in a manner similar to orchestra members and their conductor to make school reform work. Effective communication enhances satisfaction in the *S/TE* ratio of classroom teachers.

23. Reform leaders in school organizations should not use classroom teachers' private time such as lunch time or free-period time for reform activities. Teachers require this time during the school day to recover from the physical demands of teaching. Teachers are rightfully resentful of attempts to use this time for organizational goals. Time-sensitive school leaders should be respectful of teachers' private time during the school day.

24. Reform leaders should lead by the motto "Those who know the 'why' of the school reform effort can be brought to endure any 'how' needed to service the school reform effort." Convincing classroom teachers of the "why" should be the top priority. This motto is another way of convincing teachers that the school reform effort is worth their time—that is, the $S/TE$ ratio is high enough to ensure participation.

25. There is little disputing the fact that each year classroom teaching is getting far more difficult for teachers. Students are coming to school with physical, emotional, and learning problems that were not encountered in previous decades. There is a need to reform simply because students have changed in ways that make the teaching experience of little value in certain areas of the curriculum. Even though there is clearly a need for reform, convincing experienced and dedicated teachers to become involved has generally failed. Could it be that these teachers remain unconvinced that the proposed reforms are needed in their classrooms? Or could it be that they simply don't want to provide the time? The answer is probably both—with more emphasis on the latter. For this reason, reform efforts that generate from classroom teachers themselves should be taken far more seriously by the leadership in the school because these will have the highest probability of implementation.

Note that many of these recommendations to enhance teacher participation and investment in school reform activities are based on the principle of the $S/TE$ ratio. School organizations, like the economy around them, also feel the effect of time with regard to devaluation. The devaluation of social worth in school organizations such as institutional memory, tradition, loyalty, curriculum, and expertise is similar to the devaluation of economic worth in society via the inflation rate.

Time linkages are important for classroom teachers. They keep one in touch with events of previous periods of education and provide decision-making mechanisms for present teaching practices that ensure their vision for a future. With the possible exception of the teenage years, where the individual seeks an identity that is separate from the past (parents), our connection with the past or with tradition provides important meaning for what we do in the present. In essence, my life is worth something to the future and, therefore, it is important to control my behavior in the present. *The classroom teacher time linkage with the past in a school organization enhances the spirit of the workplace by continuing traditions that the organization has developed and has found to be "classical" or effective over time.*

The recent shift in time focus in school organizations from the past to the future is troublesome because the devaluation of a teacher's memory or traditions and the past results in little need for the control over a teacher's behavior in the present. Correspondingly, if the past is devalued (memory), then there is little need for future time investment of teachers because someday it, too, will become the past. Finally, nothing that lasts over time is valued in a culture of an organization that devalues the past or its traditions. Given these temporal devaluations, one should not expect an inspired sense of a future from classroom teachers whose behaviors in the present have no time link to either the past or the future. Linkages and connectivity through time—past, present, and future—therefore, form an important basis for school organizational culture and traditions. What you do in the classroom as today's teacher builds on the lives of other classroom teachers who taught before you.

Unfortunately, many classroom teachers live in communities and work in school organizations where everything around them has been devalued over time.

*Economic worth.* The dollar is worth less and less over time as teachers work harder for less and less real material compensation. The standard of living for a teacher then declines (economic devaluation).

*Subject matter.* Curriculum time compression forces more and more subject matter material to be taught by classroom teachers in less and less time (attainment devaluation). This forces teachers to accelerate their pace of instruction and invest large quantities of time to stay current.

*Expertise.* Rapid changes in the technologies of delivering instruction makes experience worth less and less to a school organization. Technological obsolescence is a trend in school organizations that ensures the devaluation of tradition (devaluation of expertise).

*Loyalty.* With rapid school reform and change, school organizations become more transitory and "bottom line" oriented. This tendency then produces a free agent view of the teaching profession (devaluation of loyalty) and the resulting behavior of the teachers is oriented only toward the present and "what's in it for me."

*Tradition.* Discrediting past knowledge as having no relevance to present problems destroys the need for tradition in the school organization. If tradition is removed, then a framework for personal behavior of teachers within the organization is also removed (devaluation of tradition). With no memory as temporal anchors, teachers are left to define their own traditions in the school organization.

*Institutional memory.* Related to the devaluation of tradition is the devaluation of institutional memory. This means that there is no memory of past organizational failures and successes and that only vision for a future based on the ideas of current leadership is possible (devaluation of the institutional memory). This type of devaluation makes the school leaders themselves into free agents, and when they leave the school organization, the reforms they have instituted also leave.

## Some Radical Strategies to
## Encourage Teacher Participation in Reform

It has been suggested in the research literature that some radical redesigns of both instructional delivery and compensation of classroom teachers would have to be implemented to free time for classroom teachers to make a career commitment and time investment to school reform and change.

In the spirit of strategies for radical change for increasing teacher commitment and time investment, the following ideas are proposed.

### Reduce Class Size to
### Increase Satisfaction and Lower Time Effort

For classroom teachers, reducing class size has typically been a strategy for increasing their classroom satisfaction while lowering their time effort. Unfortunately, attaining lower class sizes traditionally meant more teachers and thus higher school budgets. With the use of modern technology, however, one can obtain different configurations of instructional delivery that can effectively be used to reduce class sizes while maintaining similar cost.

To begin, instructional delivery would have to be modified, rooms would have to be redesigned, and computer laboratories designed to support the new instructional delivery format. For example, one type of system would be based on 30 students per class with three regular teachers (A-B-C). Each teacher would then divide each class with three groups of 10 students each (1-2-3). The idea of this type of instructional delivery design would be to maximize instructional class time while reducing class sizes and keeping within school organizational budget constraints.

As an example of how recently developed multimedia technology can be used to reduce class size and rethink our methods of instructional delivery, suppose a reform is suggested that is based on the notion of three work stations or instructional clusters for classroom instruction: small group instruction (SGI) cluster, drill practice (DP) cluster, and evaluation and diagnosis (ED) cluster.

In SGI, the class size would be 10:1, whereas the DP and ED groups would be 30 students each and be heavily oriented around multimedia technology and instructional support personnel.

Table 6.4 shows how one type of design could work in an actual school organizational setting with a 6-day instructional block and three 30-student elementary school classrooms (A-B-C). First, each 30-student classroom would have to be divided into three groups (e.g., A1, A2, and A3) of 10 students each.

---

The idea of redesigning instructional delivery is to release some formal teacher contract time for school reform and change while maintaining the integrity of the instructional delivery.

---

Naturally, other types of configurations and instructional delivery designs could be used by school organizations in an effort to

**TABLE 6.4** Alternative Block Schedule, Elementary School

|  | Monday and Tuesday | | | Wednesday and Thursday | | Friday and Monday | |
|---|---|---|---|---|---|---|---|
| Small-group instruction (10:1; three teachers, A, B, and C) | A1 | B1 | C1 | A2 B2 | C2 | A3 B3 | C3 |
| Drill practice group (30:1; add teacher's aide, technology, and workbooks) | A2 B2 C2 | | A2 B2 C2 | A3 B3 C3 | A3 B3 C3 | A1 B1 C1 | A1 B1 C1 |
| Evaluation and diagnosis group (30:1; add teacher's aide and technology-based formative evaluation) | A3 B3 C3 | | A3 B3 C3 | A1 B1 C1 | A1 B1 C1 | A2 B2 C2 | A2 B2 C2 |

increase satisfaction and reduce the time effort of classroom teachers. The idea of redesigning instructional delivery is to release some formal teacher contract time for school reform and change while maintaining the integrity of the instructional delivery in terms of overall student contact time.

## Change in Compensation Schemes for Classroom Teachers

The fixed-step salary schedule, as noted earlier, is an antiquated holdover from the early days of school organizations where highest academic degree plus college credits and years of experience were all that mattered in terms of teacher compensation. The fixed-step salary schedule was objective, easy to communicate, and based on the premise that the experience and highest academic degree of teachers best served the needs of the school organization. Naturally, the material compensation incentives for classroom teachers were to use their extra time to pile up college units, college degrees, and years of experience even if these efforts often had nothing whatever to do with improving the instruction of children. Because there were no guidelines to restrict the types or quality of these additional college units and higher degrees, school organizations were locked into a compensation scheme that was mainly ineffective in getting teachers to participate in any extra time-consuming activities of the school organization. In fact, college credit and diploma mills were packaged and set up by many private college specifically to provide teachers with these units and degrees (high *S/TE* ratios for the teacher) even if they meant nothing in terms of enhancing the legitimacy and visibility of the school organization.

It is extremely difficult for educational leaders to change the rules of the game and get teachers to provide the needed extra time investment without some sort of material compensation in this era of time scarcity. Thus, teacher compensation schemes that merely provide incentives for teachers toward obtaining degrees and college credits (in anything) now seem illogical in a modern reform-minded school organization.

### Reliance on Substitute Teachers

The literature of the school reform movement has always recognized the problem of time scarcity by classroom teachers as being the major stumbling block to school reform. A great deal of this literature proposes solutions in the area of relieving teachers of their classroom responsibilities or contract time so that they could participate in school reform activities during the school day. A substitute teacher would then carry the burden of the instructional program in the teacher's absence. Unfortunately, this type of "replacement" compensation strategy places the regular classroom teacher in a situation of having to prepare substitute teacher lesson plans and make up any class work on his or her return to the classroom. Substitute teacher replacement also places additional financial burdens on already financially desperate school organizations. Because there are only 180 instructional days in the school year, parents might also be upset that their children might have a large number of school days where substitute teachers deliver the instructional program.

As one teacher-training student noted when reflecting back on her high school experience,

> When I was a senior in high school the school administration wanted to apply for a large grant to reorganize its math curriculum. To write the proposal, the school used regular classroom

teachers and met on school time. This left substitute teachers to deliver instruction in my classes. My regular teacher, who was a wonderful teacher, was gone two or three times per week for an entire semester while he worked with other teachers to prepare the grant proposal. I felt that I was cheated out of my education and my learning was impaired. While my teacher and the other regular teachers were supposedly preparing for the needs of future students, I was being shortchanged in the present.

This student then went on to describe, in fairly typical words, the instructional quality of the substitute teachers she had that year:

When the substitute teacher was teaching our class, it became a completely different type of class. In fact, the class became more of a study hall or free day, and there was little structure or incentive for learning. Even though the substitute was supposed to have a lesson plan from the regular teacher, most of the substitutes (there were about five of them) taught to their strengths. There was a large deviation from what the regular teacher was expecting to be taught and what was actually taught. As long as we behaved ourselves, the substitute teacher let us do our own thing. Instead of a year of education, I received only a few months. My parents were quite upset, since they paid for my education through their taxes. They don't do this in private or well-run public schools.

### Substitute Teacher Pools

Related to the design for freeing up regular classroom teacher time during the regular day by the use of substitute teachers is the use of pools of substitute teachers on specific days of the week or month. By developing a pool of substitute teachers, time for reform and change by regular teachers would be guaranteed. These contract substitute classroom teachers work on specific days of the school week at a lower pay rate than regular teachers. For many highly qualified former teachers who would like to work 1 or 2 days per week, this type of teaching position would be ideal. These contract subs would be highly trained by the school organization to fill in for the regular teacher with little or no degradation in instructional delivery.

By being trained and integrated into regular instructional delivery, these teachers could substitute when a teacher is absent because of illness or when a teacher is involved in a school reform or change effort. The present warehousing of students by substitute teachers when the regular teacher is absent would thus be eliminated. In addition, the time-intensive substitute teacher lesson plan provided by the regular teacher would largely be eliminated. An empirical study that demonstrates the cost savings to the school organization of a substitute teacher pool can be found in Bruno (1970).

## Direct Instructional Downtime Compensation

Another suggestion commonly found in the school reform literature is to compensate teachers for their participation and time investment during intersessions and summer. Unfortunately, this option severely limits participation in school reform activities to certain periods of time during the year, and it is also costly to the school organization. In addition, this type of time replacement strategy results in taking away the needed "recovery" time of classroom teachers. Finally, not all teachers would participate during their free time from instruction, and the school organization would be right back where it started with limited teacher participation in school reform efforts.

## School Organization Profit Sharing

Some novel ways of compensating classroom teachers in an era of school reform were reported in the Commons Commission report for the state of California (see "Policy Initiatives," 1986). One scheme involved a profit-sharing type of compensation scheme for classroom teachers. The proposal is similar in nature to those found in high-tech industries that have large numbers of professionals and have to rely on reform and change as a matter of doing business. An adaptation of this type of "bonus" scheme was proposed where teachers as a group were paid, in addition to their regular salaries, for forming collegial teams to ensure the attainment of certain school district objectives. The idea was to get other teachers at a school site, not school leaders, to provide professional peer pressure for teachers to participate and invest in change activities because they were all in the same "compensation boat." The compensation itself was not a linear type of bonus or a one-for-one type of payment scheme but was based on a nonlinear curve compensation type scheme that reflected the degree of difficulty of the instructional environment. The *S/TE* ratio for the instructional program was then incorporated into the design of the compensation package. The problem with this type of scheme, however, is that teachers must agree to participate and the school organization has to set precisely defined goals for classroom teachers to meet.

### Redesign the Career Versus Contract Teacher

Another proposal suggested from the research reported in this book would be to change the fixed-step salary schedule itself. This new type of salary schedule would have a dual system of compensation. Essentially, one branch of the salary schedule would be for regular contract teachers with an 8 a.m. to 3 p.m. teaching assignment, and another branch of the compensation scheme would be for "career" teachers with an 8 a.m. to 5 p.m. contract. Although the 8-3 contract teachers would have to put in the time, take the additional units, and acquire higher academic degrees to move up on the salary schedule, the career 8-5 teacher would, by working a longer day, automatically move up the scale in both units and degrees. This type of time compensation proposal of a dual fixed-step schedule would be particularly appropriate to schools in most need of school reform and change and for difficult-to-staff schools. It would redefine the contract teaching day and redefine how a teacher advances in the school organization on the salary schedule. The downside would be that it might be a nontransferable benefit (except by arrangement) or form of compensation with other school districts.

### Change in the Length of the Teaching Contract

The typical fixed-step salary schedule compensates classroom teachers based on years of teaching experience and highest academic degree, and the duration of the contract is a 9-month time period. Suppose classroom teachers, like others in the workforce, could be placed on a 12-month teaching contract with a paid vacation time. Naturally, options would still be made available for classroom teachers desiring to work on a 9-month teaching contract. These extra 2 months of professional teacher time could then be used to serve the time needs of school reform. The downside would, of course, be larger school budgets for teacher salaries, and many teachers who should be involved in reform efforts would still opt out of the 12-month teaching contract. How would school organizations be able to pay teachers for the extra 3 months? This might be a role for the federal government in public education—namely, to subsidize the school reform movement at the local school organization level. The problem of getting all teachers to commit for 12 months might be far more problematic, especially for older teachers who have come to plan other activities around these 3 months.

## Miscellaneous Suggestions

There have been other suggestions for providing needed classroom teacher time to service school reform efforts. One suggestion is to add to the school calendar formal meeting days devoted specifically to reform. This would free all teachers to work on planning for reform and change within the 9-month teaching contract. The number of instructional days, however, would be shortened, and this might lead to public opposition.

Another option would be to slightly increase class size and with the extra money generated, pay for additional long-term substitute teachers. While regular classroom teachers would be engaged in school reform efforts, these substitute teachers would be called on to deliver the instructional program.

Suggestions have also been proposed to lengthen the school day Monday through Thursday, then have a half-day of classroom instruction on Friday. Friday afternoons would then be devoted to school reform and change.

Finally, there is a popular expression: "If I had 8 hours to chop down a tree, I would use 6 in sharpening the ax." This proverb strongly suggests that it might be far better for educational leadership to understand teacher resistance to organizational change and the extra time needs of school reform before imposing reform change on unwilling participants.

# Summary

*It's About Time* has attempted to establish the following key points with regard to understanding teacher behaviors toward time investments in school change and reform.

• For classroom teachers and school organizations, time acts like a bridge that links the past (traditions and memories), the present (classroom behavior), and the future (vision and expectations).

• Teachers use their time for two extremely important purposes that are of critical importance to classroom learning: time to establish the persona that they wear in the school organization as a classroom teacher, for example, subject matter specialist or general classroom educator, and time needed to find the self or what is referred to in this book as lifestyle satisfaction.

• The sense of time control in the lifetime of a classroom teacher is a major nonpecuniary benefit for teachers that will tend to erode in coming years as charter schools, magnet schools, alternative schools, and private schools emerge as methods for delivering educational services. This major nonpecuniary benefit of time presents and has presented options for teachers so that they could make various types of alternative time investment decisions related to personal goals of lifestyle satisfaction. In the coming years, the issue of time control of classroom teachers, more than salary levels, might be a major concern in collective bargaining negotiations.

• The important management-of-change principle of the satisfaction or worth or benefits received for the time effort expended is strongly related to the propensity of an individual teacher to participate and invest in the extra time-consuming activities of the school organization. Educational leaders have to appreciate teachers' concern regarding the question, "Is the activity worth my time?" and develop proactive strategies for increasing satisfaction ($S$) and lowering the time effort ($TE$) associated with the activity. The $S/TE$ ratio not only relates to participation and investment in the extra time-consuming activities of the school organization but also relates to teacher behaviors observed in the classroom itself such as burnout, dropout, commitment, and pushout.

• Time is an important resource needed from classroom teachers by the school organization to promote school reform and change. Time is a core value, and as such there is simply no choice but for educational leaders to understand and appreciate the role that time plays in the lifetimes of teachers and the evolutionary life of the school organization. Unhappy teachers will make their presence felt in the school organization and can cause great harm to attaining educational objectives. In addition, although educational leaders might design the reform activity, it is up to classroom teachers to deliver the reform to students.

• Educational leaders often view older teachers' behaviors as being different from younger teachers' behaviors. These differences are particularly acute with regard to their willingness to commit extra time to the reform and change process. This situation could be related to the subjective weighted hour of time between the two groups of teachers. For example , the difference in the sense of scarcity of a 1-hour time investment for an older teacher is greater than the sense of time scarcity for a younger teacher.

• Loyalty of teachers to the school organization is built on memories accumulated over long time periods. For classroom teachers, memory of the past and vision for a future affect their present behavior in the classroom. By eliminating or devaluing the memory of older teachers and correspondingly overvaluing the values of younger teachers, educational leaders are placed in a precarious position of designing school reforms that might not be amenable to the actual classroom teaching situation and be misled in designing school reforms.

• The numerous waves of proposed school reforms in the United States have generally failed to effectively reform schools because most of these reforms required more teacher time effort while satisfaction either remained the same or was lowered. Future school reforms will be compared to those that failed in the past, and unless time and the *S/TE* ratio are considered, classroom teachers will conclude that the reform is not worth the time.

• The cyclical time frame perspective of the school organization and the linear time frame perspective of the classroom teacher create major problems for educational leaders interested in change and reform. Incentives for time investment are created for teachers who teach the same subject matter each year to front-load their "school-teaching-related" time investments in their early career, and then, if they choose, glide for the rest of their career in the classroom. Ownership of the curriculum and subject matter or courses by teachers is related to time and time investments made in the past.

• Effective teachers are and have always been important to the educational process because they teach their "selves" to their students, rather than their subject matter. Happy and productive teachers who sense control of their time in a lifetime, and who are pursuing their goals of lifestyle satisfaction, are far more important for promoting classroom learning than any school reform effort.

• Classroom teachers appear to be extraordinarily different (e.g., male or female, elementary or secondary, young or old, etc.) regarding their perceptions of time and the time investments they are willing to "give" or "sell" to the school organization. Any uniform educational leadership policy for creating incentives for teachers to invest extra time in the school organization would, therefore, be largely ineffectual.

• Finally, educational leaders in an era of time scarcity need to view teacher compensation or perceived benefits (i.e., satisfaction) for time investments from a broader perspective to include not only material compensation but, even more important for older teachers, social and psychological personal development compensation. Correspondingly, time effort expectations from teachers will have to be reexamined in the context of time scarcity in society and modern time compression and time-saving devices that are available to the school organization.

In conclusion, the quality of the lifetime of a teacher is highly related to the teacher's personal perception of time. *The important role that time plays in the lifetime of a teacher and the evolution of the school organization suggests ways in which both lifestyle satisfaction goals of the teacher and organizational legitimacy goals of the school organization can be attained in a win-win framework.* Improving the quality of the lifetime of a teacher, using some of the time principles and ideas presented in these chapters, will potentially have more impact on student learning than the implementation of the school reform effort itself. Understanding and appreciating the fascinating and complex nature of time as a currency of exchange between the classroom teacher and the school organization are important first steps for educational leaders in an era of time scarcity.

## Perspectives, Points of View, Discussion

- In what ways do you feel some of the proposed redesigns of instructional delivery, as suggested by recent school reforms, might affect the control of classroom teacher time in your school organization?
- What do you feel will be the time role of a classroom teacher in the future as a result of some of the school reforms that are now being planned?
- How can teacher loyalty be maintained across both younger and older teachers in school organizations that are undergoing reform and change?
- How do you propose to increase classroom teacher satisfaction or benefits from the school reforms you are currently proposing?
- How do you propose to lower time effort for classroom teachers with the school reforms you are now proposing?
- Have the various waves of school reforms over the past several decades lowered your confidence and expectations regarding the effectiveness of recent school reform efforts?
- What are some of the mechanisms you can suggest to increase participation rates and time investments of classroom teachers?

## NOTE

1. This quote is from a personal interview.

# References

Adam, B. (1990). *Time and social theory.* Cambridge, UK: Polity.

Alley, R. (1990). Moonlighting teachers leave reform efforts in the dark. *School Administrator, 47*(7), 21.

Bardwick, J. (1986). *The plateauing trap.* New York: American Management Association.

Becker, H. S. (1960). Notes on the concept of commitment. *American Journal of Sociology, 66,* 32-42.

Bell, D., & Roach, P. (1990). Moonlighting: The economic reality of teaching. *Education, 10*(3), pp. 397-402.

Ben-Peretz, M., & Bromme, R. (Eds.). (1990). *The nature of time in schools.* New York: Teachers College Press.

Bluedorn, A. C., & Denhardt, R. B. (1988). Time and organizations. *Journal of Management, 14,* 299-320.

Bolman, L. G., & Deal, T. E. (1984). *Modern approaches to understanding and managing organizations.* San Francisco: Jossey-Bass.

Bonaparte, M. (1940). Time and the unconscious. *International Journal of Psycho-Analysis, 21,* 427-468.

Braxton, G. (1986, April 16). Teachers vote to boycott open house in Burbank. *Los Angeles Times,* p. 6.

Bruno, J. E. (1970). Use of Monte Carlo analysis to determine optimal size of substitute teacher pools. *Journal of Socio-Economic Planning Sciences, 4,* 415-428.

Bruno, J. E. (1995). Doing time-killing time at school: An examination of the perceptions and allocations of time among teacher defined at-risk students. *Urban Review, 27*(2), 101-120.

Bruno, J. E., & Maguire, S. R. (1993). Perception and allocation of time by dyslexic children. *Perceptual and Motor Skills, 77,* 419-432.

Colarusso, C. (1994). *Fulfillment in adulthood: Paths to the pinnacle of life.* New York: Plenum.

Cottle, T. (1967). The circles test: An investigation of perceptions and temporal relatedness. *Journal of Projective Techniques and Personality Measurement, 31*(5), 58-71.

Cottle, T. (1976). *Perceiving time.* New York: John Wiley.

Crowe, P. H. (1978). *How to teach school and make a living at the same time.* Kansas City, MO: Andrews & McMeel.

Cushman, P. (1990). Why the self is empty: Towards an historically situated psychology. *American Psychologist, 45*(5), 599-611.

Cutler, A. B., & Ruopp, F. N. (1993, March). Buying time for teachers. *Professional Development Educational Leadership,* pp. 34-37.

Donahoe, T. (1993). Finding the way: Structure, time, and culture in school improvement. *Phi Delta Kappan, 6,* 298-305.

Douglass, M. E., & Douglass, D. N. (1980). *Manage your time, manage your work, manage yourself.* New York: Amacom.

Eisner, E. (1992). Educational reform and the ecology of schooling. *Teachers College Record, 93,* 610-627.

Enriquez, S., & Gordon, L. (1989, May 25). Talks resume in teachers' strike; end may be in sight. *Los Angeles Times,* p. A1.

Fortman, Z. E. (1984). *The role and perceived stress of secondary school administrators in year-round and traditional schools.* Unpublished doctoral dissertation, University of California, Los Angeles.

Fraser, J. T. (Ed.). (1981). *The voices of time* (2nd ed.). Amherst: University of Massachusetts Press.

Friedman, W. J. (1990). *The developmental psychology of time.* New York: Academic Press.

Fullan, M., & Miles, M. (1992). Getting reform right: What works and what doesn't work. *Phi Delta Kappan, 73,* 744-753.

Gandera, P. (1992). Extended year, extended contracts: Increasing teacher salary options. *Urban Education, 27,* 229-247.

Greenberg, S. F. (1984). *Stress and the teaching profession.* Baltimore: Paul H. Brookes.

Hannaway, J., & Carnoy, M. (1993). *Decentralization and school improvement: Can we fulfill the promise.* San Francisco: Jossey-Bass.

Hargraves, A. (1992). Time and teachers' work: An analysis of the intensification thesis. *Teachers College Record, 94*(1), 87-108.

Hassard, J. (1991). Aspects of time in organizations. *Human Relation, 44*(2), 105-124.

Heirich, M. (1964). The use of time in the study of social change. *American Sociological Review, 24,* 386-397.

Henderson, D. (1994, April). *Texas teachers, moonlighting and morale.* (ERIC Microfiche Collection No. ED 369 744)

Howard, A., & Bray, D. (1988). *Managerial lives in transition: Advancing age and changing times.* New York: Guilford Press.

Johansen, J. J. (1992). Some characteristics associated with effectiveness of elementary school principals as demonstrated by role perceptions and the utilization of time. *Dissertation Abstracts International, 44*(7-A).

Leigh, P. J. (1986). Accounting for tastes: correlates of risk and time preferences. *Journal of Post Keynesian Economics, 9*(1), 17-31.

Lewis, D., & Weigert, A. (1981). The structure and meaning of social time. *Social Forces, 60*(2), 450-455.

Lomranz, J., Friedman, A., Gitter, G., Shmotkin, D., & Medini, G. (1985). The meaning of time related concepts across a lifespan. *International Journal of Aging and Human Development, 21*(2), 87-107.

Lortie, D. (1975). *School teacher.* Chicago: University of Chicago Press.

Marcano, T. (1990, May 2). Letter from district warns teacher that homework ban violates contract. *Los Angeles Times,* p. B9.

Maslow, A. H. (1943). A theory of human motivation. *Psychological Review, 50*(4), 370-396.

Maslow, A. H. (1970). *Motivation and personality* (2nd ed.). New York: Harper and Row. (Original work published 1954)

Massey, M. (1979). *The people puzzle: Understanding yourself and others.* Reston, VA: Reston.

McGrath, J. E., & Rotchford, N. L. (1983). Time and behavior in organizations. *Research in Organizational Behavior, 5,* 57-101.

Milstein, M. (1990a). The implications of educator plateauing for staff development. *Journal of Personnel Evaluation in Education, 3,* 325-326.

Milstein, M. (1990b). Plateauing as an occupational phenomenon among teachers and administrators. *Journal of Staff Development, 2*(1), 48-52.

National Education Association, Research Division. (1992). *Status of the American public school teacher 1990-1991.* Washington, DC: Author.

Nemiroff, R. A., & Colarusso, C. A. (1985). *The race against time.* New York: Plenum.

O'Connor, D. J. & Woolfe, D. M. (1987). On managing midlife transitions in career and family. *Journal of Human Relations, 12,* 799-816.

Policy initiatives for developing a teaching profession [Special issue]. (1986) *Elementary School Journal, 86*(4).

Purnell, S., & Hill, P. (1992). *Time for reform* (RAND report). Santa Monica, CA: RAND.

Raywid, M. A. (1993). Finding time for collaboration. *Educational Leadership, 51*(1), 30-34.

Rousseau, P. M. (1989). Psychological and implied contracts in organizations. *Employee Rights and Responsibilities Journal, 2,* 121-139.

Sarason, S. B. (1990). *The predictable failure of educational reform.* San Francisco: Jossey-Bass.

Sharp, C. (1981). *The economics of time.* New York: Halsted.

Shmotkin, D. (1991). The role of time orientation in life satisfaction across the life span. *Journal of Gerontology, 46*(5), 234-250.

Smith, J. (1995). *Latino gang male youth and risk factors: Time allocations, time perceptions and locus of control.* Unpublished doctoral dissertation, University of California, Los Angeles.

Stark, J. S., Lowther, M. A., & Austin, A. E. (1985). Teachers preferred time allocation: Can it be predicted? *Journal of Experimental Education, 53,* 170-183.

Time is not on their side. (1989, February 27). *Time,* p. 7.

Watkins, P. (1993). Finding time: Temporal considerations in the organization for school committees. *British Journal of Sociology, 14*(2), 131-146.

Watts, G. D., & Castle, S. (1993). The time dilemma in school restructuring. *Phi Delta Kappan, 75,* 306-310.

West, F. (1990). Educational collaboration and restructuring of schools. *Journal of Educational and Psychological Consultation, 1*(1), 23-40.

Woo, E. (1989, May 14). Two men and three major issues snarl L.A. school talks. *Los Angeles Times,* pp. A1-A2, A7.

Zerubavel, E. (1981). *Hidden rhythms: Schedules and calendars in everyday life.* Chicago: University of Chicago Press.

# Index

CORWIN
PRESS